Attention Deficit Hyperactivity Disorder

Questions & Answers for Parents

Gregory S. Greenberg
Wade F. Horn

Research Press
2612 North Mattis Avenue • Champaign, Illinois 61821

Cover design by Elizabeth D. Burczy, Chicago, Illinois
Composition by Wadley Graphix Corporation
Printed by McNaughton & Gunn, Inc.

ISBN 0-87822-322-3
Library of Congress Catalog No. 91-61551

Contents

86051

Figures

Acknowledgments

Although it would be impossible for us to thank all who
have contributed to the development of this book, several persons deserve special mention for their inspiration
and helpfulness. First, we wish to thank our mentors,
Drs. Russell Barkley, C. Keith Connors, James O'Donnell,
and Karen Wells, without whom our understanding of
children with Attention Deficit Hyperactivity Disorder
would be inadequate to the task of writing this book.
We also wish to thank the many graduate students and
colleagues who unselfishly dedicated their time and effort
to the Child Behavior Project, a clinical research program at
Michigan State University for the treatment of children with
ADHD, where many of the ideas contained in this book
were first put to the test. Special acknowledgment is
reserved for Nicholas Ialongo, Ph.D., Jack Pascoe, M.D.,
Michael Lopez, and Thomas Packard, Ph.D., whose con-
tributions to the Child Behavior Project were numerous
and invaluable. We also want to express our gratitude to
Dr. Michael Rothenberg and Jo Rothenberg for their
encouragement and advice concerning the publication of
this book, and to Reed Martin, J.D., for his help in answering the question concerning the school's legal responsibilities toward the child with ADHD. Finally, the first author
would like to thank Bridget, and the second author would
like to thank Claudia, Christen, and Caroline for their patience, understanding, and support during the writing of
this book.

Introduction

Your child has just been diagnosed as having Attention Deficit Hyperactivity Disorder. What does that mean, and what can you do to help? In our clinical practice over the last decade, parents have asked us these and countless other questions about ADHD. Written in a readable question-and-answer format, this book attempts to address the questions parents ask most frequently and gives concrete ideas you can use to help your child with ADHD lead a happier and more productive life.

Today, more children than ever before are being diagnosed as having ADHD. However, ADHD is not really a new development. In the mid-1800s, reports began to appear in the medical literature of children having chronic problems with impulsiveness, overactivity, and inattentiveness. Although these reports have persisted over the years, tremendous controversy exists about the causes for such problems. Indeed, there has even been disagreement over what to call children with these difficulties. Such terms as "minimal brain damage," "minimal brain dysfunction," "hyperactive child syndrome," and "hyperkinetic reaction of childhood" have all been applied to these children. Each has been discarded as new information about the disorder has been discovered. Most recently, children with the chronic problems just described have been classified as either having Attention Deficit Disorder (with or without hyperactivity) or as having Attention Deficit Hyperactivity Disorder.

In addition to controversy regarding the causes and classification of what is now known as ADHD, disagreement exists surrounding its appropriate treatment. (There is even a minority view that ADHD does not really exist and that specific medications, behavior management, and talk therapies are therefore inappropriate!) Although we acknowledge this considerable disagreement, the preponderance of research evidence over the past 25 years suggests that medication and behavior management are the most effective treatments for the disorder and that talk therapies can be useful when combined with these approaches. A physician must evaluate the appropriateness of the use of medication, and talk therapies are best undertaken by a trained mental health professional. However, you can do a great deal to help your child by having the most up-to-date information about ADHD and by putting into practice the various behavioral techniques described in this book.

The specific techniques we suggest here are based upon the assumption that behavior is learned and that, by creating the best possible environment for learning, parents and others in the child's environment can have a tremendous impact on how the child deals with the challenge of ADHD. Many books discuss the application of behavioral principles with children—and a number of these are included in this volume's bibliography and reference list. This book is different, however, because it selects the specific techniques that are most helpful for children with ADHD and explains why they can be particularly effective for this group. Research has shown that such techniques can teach children to get along better with others, provide the structure children need to follow directions and complete activities, and change the negative patterns of family interaction that so often develop over a period of years.

Chapters 1 and 2 cover questions about the problems most often observed in children with ADHD and about effective, currently available treatments. In chapters 3 through 8, we answer questions concerning the particular behavioral techniques found useful in helping the child with ADHD. Chapter 9 deals with questions about teenagers who have ADHD, and chapter 10 responds to parents' concerns about school behavior problems. Finally, in chapter 11 we summarize the techniques parents can use in "troubleshooting" if future problems arise.

Of course, very complex behavioral programs are best undertaken with the help of an experienced mental health professional. But parents can make profound changes simply by creating a situation that minimizes frustrations and makes activities and interactions more pleasurable.

Given this type of situation, children with ADHD can and do succeed. These successes in turn provide the framework for the kind of self-esteem that will serve them well throughout life.

CHAPTER ONE

Overview

What is Attention Deficit Hyperactivity Disorder?

Attention Deficit Hyperactivity Disorder, often referred to as ADHD or simply as hyperactivity, is characterized by difficulties with inattention, impulsivity, and overactivity. Children with the disorder have difficulty paying attention, tend to act quickly without thinking things through, and have trouble sitting still for lengthy periods. In addition, these difficulties have been present, at least to some degree, since the child was 7 years old or younger, and they have existed for at least 6 months. In other words, a child cannot suddenly develop ADHD; rather, indications or signs of the disorder must have been present for a relatively long time. Children with ADHD generally display some difficulty in the three areas of inattention, impulsivity, and overactivity, but in varying proportions. That is, some children might be quite inattentive and impulsive but show little overactivity; others might be very overactive as well as inattentive and impulsive. This is one of the most confusing aspects of the disorder—no two children with ADHD look exactly alike.

How many children have ADHD?

ADHD is one of the most common reasons for referral to child mental health services in this country. Indeed, according to surveys of the literature by Trites, Dugas, Lynch, and Ferguson in 1979 and LaGreca and Quay in 1984, children with ADHD account for a substantial percentage of all child referrals to outpatient mental health clinics in the United States. Estimates of the overall prevalence of ADHD vary, but, according to the American Psychiatric Association's (1987) *Diagnostic and Statistical Manual of Mental Disorders,* up to 3 percent of children suffer from it. This means that approximately one child in every classroom in the United States has ADHD.

I've heard that more boys than girls have ADHD. How come?

It is quite true that more boys than girls have ADHD. In fact, Szatmari, Offord, and Boyle (1989), as well as Trites, Dugas, Lynch, and Ferguson (1979), found that approximately three times as many boys as girls possess ADHD. In addition, the *Diagnostic and Statistical Manual of Mental Disorders* notes that ADHD is six to nine times more common in boys than in girls. However, it is not known why ADHD is more common among boys than among girls. What is known is that boys tend to be more at risk for developing almost any childhood behavioral or emotional problem. That is, boys seem to be more vulnerable during the early developmental years to a wide range of difficulties—one of which is ADHD.

What are the signs of ADHD?

The most important feature of ADHD is *difficulty focusing and maintaining attention* on a task or activity without being distracted. At home, attentional problems are often characterized by difficulty following directions, complying with requests, completing chores and homework assignments, and playing alone for extended periods. At school, children with ADHD are often described by their teachers as having difficulty paying attention in class, completing in-seat assignments in a timely manner, and following directions. These children are often easily distracted from schoolwork by schoolmates or by activities that are irrelevant to the assigned task.

Some parents and teachers believe that if a child can pay attention to activities like video games and TV, then that child cannot have ADHD. However, this is not necessarily true. Some children with ADHD are, in fact, very capable of concentrating on activities such as video games and TV—often for long periods. These same children, however, have much greater difficulty than most children their age in concentrating and maintaining effort when it comes to such things as doing homework, completing chores, and following directions. That's because children with ADHD are thought to have much more trouble concentrating and maintaining effort when the task is imposed on them by someone else—for instance, a parent or a teacher—than when they choose the task and it appeals to them. The reason for this is not known. Perhaps it is unusually hard for children with ADHD to maintain their attention and effort on tasks that they find boring and unmotivating, whereas other children have a greater tolerance for and ability to perform such tasks. That is, children with ADHD, compared to other children, may have more difficulty motivating themselves to do well on tasks they find uninteresting.

The second most important feature of ADHD is *difficulty delaying impulses.* Children with ADHD often act before thinking about the possible consequences of their actions. For example, they may speak out in class without being called on, may show carelessness on a schoolwork problem by answering it hastily without thinking it through, may have difficulty waiting their turn in a school lunch line or in a game, and may show a tendency to get into verbal and/or physical fights with others, especially when frustrated. Indeed, even when children with ADHD know the rules, they have trouble following them. In both the home and the classroom, children with ADHD often violate even the most basic rules and social conventions; as a result, they are more frequently criticized or punished than other children. In fact, this impulsiveness leads some children with ADHD to take greater physical risks than others and causes them to suffer more medical injuries than do their peers. For this reason, some parents describe their children with ADHD as accident-prone.

What about overactivity? Is this also an important characteristic of children with ADHD?

There is some controversy as to whether or not overactivity must be present for a child to be diagnosed as having ADHD. Currently, the best research suggests that not all children with ADHD are, in fact, chronically overactive and that not all children with ADHD who are overactive are overactive in all situations. That is, when overactivity is present, it is most likely to be seen when the child is in group situations that demand much concentration and attention, as well as delaying of impulses. For instance, in a classroom the child with ADHD may be excessively fidgety, may have difficulty staying in an assigned seat, and may even run about the classroom or climb on desks and chairs.

Such overactivity may also be displayed at meals, during car rides, at religious services, and in other possibly confining situations. On the playground, however, a child with ADHD may not appear more overactive than others of the same age. In addition, the activity level of the child with ADHD has been noted to decrease in new situations, but it may rise again when the child becomes more familiar with the situation. Overall, it is probably best to think of overactivity as a frequently present, but not essential, feature of ADHD.

Do children with ADHD have other significant problems?

In addition to inattention, impulsivity, and overactivity, several other symptoms are often associated with (but are not necessary for) a diagnosis of ADHD. The most important of these additional characteristics is *poor school performance*. Children with ADHD are two to three times more likely than other children to be retained at least once during grade school. In some cases, difficulty in school is the result of inattention and impulsivity problems. For example, if a child with ADHD has trouble paying attention to what the teacher is saying, it will be very difficult for that child to do well in school. Furthermore, because children with ADHD tend to be disciplined more often than their peers, they may miss a lot of classroom instruction while spending time in the hallway or in the principal's office.

Children with ADHD are also more likely than other children to suffer from a *specific learning disability*. In fact, some researchers, including Safer and Allen (1976), have found that as many as 60 to 80 percent of children with ADHD have learning disabilities in addition to their ADHD. This means that most of these children not only find it hard to pay attention in the classroom but also find it hard to process information being given by the teacher even when they *are* paying attention. In such a case, the child with ADHD is truly pulling double duty and may feel quite overwhelmed. It is easy to see why such a child can quickly become turned off to school.

A third major additional characteristic of children with ADHD is *aggressive behavior*. Such children are often described as defiant, angry, hostile, and oppositional in response to the commands of others. They may also become frustrated easily, have frequent temper tantrums, and strike out at others in response to even relatively minor provocations. In fact, many children with ADHD often are initially referred for mental health services not because of difficulties with inattention but because of aggressive behavior.

Given the difficulties these children frequently have with inattention, impulsiveness, and aggression, it should not be surprising that a fourth major additional characteristic of ADHD is *difficulty getting along with other children of the same age*. When placed in socially frustrating situations, children with ADHD are more likely than others to respond impulsively without thinking through the consequences of their actions. Often these impulsive decisions lead to aggressive or otherwise socially unacceptable behaviors. This can result in social isolation, if not outright social rejection, by peers. In fact, children with ADHD are often described as being more comfortable with younger playmates who may be more forgiving or tolerant of social misbehavior.

A fifth important additional characteristic associated with ADHD, which may or may not be present, is *difficulty with motor coordination*. Children with ADHD often appear clumsy and poorly coordinated—for example, when holding a pencil, throwing a ball, running in a race, or jumping rope. For boys in particular, clumsiness may further aggravate difficulties with forming and maintaining effective peer relationships because such boys are often excluded from, or held in poor regard when participating in, sporting activities.

Finally, as a consequence of frequent experiences of failure as well as nearly constant reprimands and criticism from others, children with ADHD often suffer from *poor self-esteem and a sense of low self-worth*. Indeed, the aggressive behavior displayed by many of these children is often the result of their becoming so frustrated that they act out by hitting, throwing temper tantrums, and the like. Others may express their frustration in different ways: by withdrawing from others, becoming depressed, or developing various body complaints such as headaches, stomachaches, and more generalized aches and pains. The child with ADHD may also attempt to avoid school activities out of fear of failing and appearing "dumb" in front of classmates.

Are these additional problems always present?

The additional characteristics just described *may* be present, but they do not have to be present for a child to have ADHD. That is, some children may have ADHD and be aggressive, whereas other children may have ADHD but not be aggressive. Some may have ADHD and a learning disability, whereas others may have ADHD but no learning disability. Again, this is one of the most confusing aspects of ADHD—no two children with ADHD are exactly alike.

When a child has so many different problems, don't the parents feel overwhelmed?

Given this rather long list of additional problematic characteristics of children with ADHD, it may not be surprising that often parents of children with ADHD do feel overwhelmed. A child's difficult temperament and behavior related to ADHD may contribute to negative parent-child interactions. Parents who are chronically made to feel incompetent by their inability to control their child's behavior or who feel unloved because of their child's constant misbehavior may be at greater risk either to express their frustration in a physically aggressive manner or to avoid the child and neglect his needs. Indeed, children with ADHD, compared to others, have a greater likelihood of being abused and/or neglected by their parents. It is important to note, however, that relatively few parents will actually abuse their child simply because the child happens to have ADHD. That is one reason why it is so important to accurately diagnose ADHD as early as possible—so that treatment can be given and the development of potentially dangerous interaction patterns between the child and the parents can be avoided.

If the additional problems that you mentioned do not have to be present for a child to be diagnosed as having ADHD, why are they important to know about?

For two reasons. First, these additional characteristics can sometimes be so prominent in a given child that underlying ADHD is overlooked. Thus, aggressive children may be labeled conduct disordered or bad when, in fact, much of their aggression stems from the frustration and failure they experience at school and at home because of their ADHD. Other children may appear very sad or depressed, and there may be no recognition that their sadness or depression is actually the result of an ADHD problem. Other children may be labeled learning disabled and given special education services that may not specifically address their difficulties with inattention.

Second, and perhaps more important, these additional characteristics affect what happens to children with ADHD as they grow up. It seems that it is not the severity of the inattention and impulsivity problems that predicts which children with ADHD will have problems later in life, but rather the presence or absence of additional symptoms. That is, children with ADHD but *without* learning disabilities, *without* aggressive behaviors, *without* peer relationship difficulties, and so on are much more likely to be relatively problem free when they are older than are children with ADHD who have learning disabilities, are aggressive, or experience poor peer relationships. That is why a good assessment for ADHD will always include measures of these additional characteristics. Where additional problems are present, treatment must address these additional characteristics as well as the underlying ADHD.

What is likely to happen to a child with ADHD as she grows up?

It was formerly believed that ADHD was primarily an early childhood problem and that, once the child became a teenager, the ADHD "went away." This was because we used to focus exclusively on the child's overactivity, which does tend to improve dramatically as the child becomes a teenager. We now know, however, that the inattentiveness and impulsiveness of children with ADHD do not simply disappear with time. Although both inattentiveness and impulsiveness do tend to get better as the child grows older, teenagers with ADHD continue to experience much greater difficulty than do other teenagers. For example, they continue to underachieve in school, are more often described as having a rebellious attitude, and are more often in conflict with authority figures. Even in adulthood, the person with ADHD, if untreated, is at greater risk for alcohol abuse, depression, and even criminal behavior.

The news is not all bad, however. In fact, according to
Barkley's (1990) assessment of research results to date, 35 to
50 percent of children with ADHD do fairly well as adults;
in other words, they do not have problems with behavior in
general or with ADHD symptoms specifically. And there is
very recent and exciting research suggesting that with proper
early treatment, children with ADHD can grow up to be
responsible, productive, successful, and happy adults—
especially if they receive a comprehensive, individualized
treatment program. Such a program could include both
medication and psychological treatment.

What causes ADHD?

ADHD has not been traced to any single cause. Rather,
there seem to be a number of possible causes. First of all,
ADHD is *not* a type of mental retardation. Children with
ADHD usually possess at least average intelligence. In addition, although in a very small percentage of these children
there is damage to the nervous system, no good evidence
exists to support the idea that children with ADHD are in
fact brain damaged. Rather, it is currently believed that ADHD
is due to an understimulation of the brain areas that enable
a child to sustain attention, delay impulsive responses,
control motor activity, follow rules, maintain motivation,
and plan behavior. Researchers have hypothesized that such
understimulation is due to dysfunction or delay in the
development of these brain areas. As a matter of fact, it has
been suggested that the overactivity sometimes seen in children with ADHD is really the body's attempt to stimulate
these areas of the brain so that they can pay attention better.

Exactly why some children have an understimulation of
these brain areas is unclear. Some believe that difficulties
during pregnancy or delivery may cause ADHD. For
example, maternal smoking, alcohol consumption, and
cocaine use during pregnancy have been found to be
associated with ADHD in children. However, it is not
possible to conclude that these maternal behaviors *cause*
ADHD. An alternative explanation is that mothers of
children with ADHD may have experienced great stress and
emotional difficulty that led them to smoke, drink, and/or
abuse drugs while pregnant. In this view, it is possible that
emotional stress during pregnancy, rather than drinking,

smoking, or drug abuse, increases the risk of ADHD. Indeed, these maternal behaviors may not cause ADHD at all, even indirectly.

Genetic factors may also play a role. For instance, some studies suggest that parents of children with ADHD are more likely to have had attentional and impulse control problems themselves when they were children. Children with ADHD have also been found to be more likely to have siblings with behavioral and emotional problems, including ADHD. Furthermore, studies of twins have generally found that an identical twin of a child with ADHD is more likely also to have ADHD than is a fraternal twin.

I've heard that sugar and food additives can cause ADHD. Is this true?

There has been much debate about whether refined sugar and food additives such as preservatives and dyes cause ADHD. Actually, there is little research supporting the idea that these substances cause ADHD in most cases. Some have suggested that when parents and teachers perceive ingestion of sugar as increasing a child's disruptive behavior, it is because ingestion of sugar often occurs during such times as school recess, family outings, and birthday parties. Thus, increases in ADHD-related behaviors may be due to participation in these relatively unstructured and highly stimulating activities rather than to the sugar itself.

It is possible, however, that such substances could worsen the behavioral symptoms of ADHD. For an analogy, suppose you have a car with a faulty carburetor. If you put the wrong kind of gasoline in the car, it will function even more poorly than if you had put in the right gasoline. However, the underlying reason the car does not run properly is that the carburetor is faulty. Thus, although the right gasoline will make the car run a bit better, it will not solve the difficulty with the carburetor. Only when you repair the carburetor will the car perform as it should. Likewise, if you give a child with ADHD food additives or refined sugars, the child may display an increase in ADHD-related behaviors. But this would not necessarily mean that the food additives or refined sugars *caused* the ADHD; rather, it could simply aggravate an already difficult problem.

I've also heard that breathing lead from car exhaust can cause ADHD. Is this true?

It has also been suggested that low levels of lead poisoning, such as those caused by breathing car exhaust fumes from leaded gasolines, is a cause of ADHD. Although it is true that some children with ADHD do have elevated levels of lead in their bodies, it is also true that many children with ADHD do not show elevated levels of lead. Thus, it seems that, although the presence of lead may be associated with increased overactivity in some children, it is probably not a major cause of ADHD.

How can I find out if my child has ADHD?

The best way to determine whether your child has ADHD is to have him evaluated by a qualified psychologist or other mental health professional who not only will assess whether your child is inattentive, impulsive, and/or overactive but also will try to determine why he has these symptoms. Assessing for alternative explanations of inattentive and impulsive behavior is important because other problems can masquerade as ADHD. For example, children who are excessively anxious or worry a lot will often be inattentive and fidgety in the classroom, and they may even be impulsive as well. In addition, some children who appear inattentive may really have a problem with language processing, hearing, or vision—that is, some children have difficulty understanding, hearing, or seeing the instructions from a teacher or a parent. Here the problem is not one of inattentiveness to instructions but of understanding, hearing, or seeing the instructions themselves.

Why is an evaluation so important?

The reason it is important to determine accurately *why* a child is having trouble with inattentiveness, impulsiveness, and/or overactivity is that different treatments are needed for different underlying problems. For example, overanxious children may need psychological counseling, whereas children with language processing problems may need special education help. Treatment for ADHD is quite different, as we will discuss later in the book.

A comprehensive evaluation is important for another reason as well. As we pointed out earlier, it is not so much the severity of the ADHD itself that predicts how children will achieve and get along in life as they grow older, but rather the presence or absence of a number of additional symptoms, such as learning disabilities, aggression, and poor peer relationships. A comprehensive evaluation is needed to determine the presence or absence of these additional symptoms, as well as to diagnose whether or not the child has ADHD. And if any additional symptoms are present, recommendations should be made for appropriate treatment to address these symptoms.

What would a comprehensive evaluation include?

A good comprehensive evaluation should do exactly what the term implies—get a well-rounded picture of your child. Such an evaluation should include measures of your child's thinking abilities (that is, an appropriate intelligence test) and academic functioning (that is, tests of reading, spelling, and arithmetic ability). It should assess social functioning (your child's ability to get along with friends, family, and community members, as well as possible cultural influences upon behavior), emotional functioning (how your child feels about herself and others), and developmental abilities (your child's capacity to perform activities of daily living that are appropriate for her age, such as getting dressed, appropriately using writing and eating utensils, showing gross and fine motor coordination, and using speech). Finally, a comprehensive evaluation should include measures of attention span and impulsivity.

That sounds like a lot. Can my pediatrician evaluate my child in the office?

Possibly—so long as the pediatrician evaluates *all* of these areas in your child. Unfortunately, most pediatricians are far too busy to spend the 3 to 4 hours necessary to establish a diagnosis, rule out alternative explanations, and evaluate for the presence or absence of additional symptoms. Also, most children with ADHD can appear perfectly symptom free for up to an hour if they are placed in a highly structured situation such as a doctor's office. We find that pediatricians are very good at screening for ADHD. However, you should arrange for a more thorough and comprehensive evaluation, one that results in a complete treatment plan for your child.

Does my child need to see only a psychologist or other mental health worker in order to receive both a diagnosis and a plan for treatment?

Although a qualified psychologist or other mental health professional is usually capable of making a comprehensive evaluation, consultation with other health care or school personnel may be necessary to adequately cover all the assessment areas mentioned earlier. If problems other than ADHD are found, then it is especially important for the psychologist to consult with other health care or school workers to ensure that your child receives appropriate care. For instance, if your child is found to have a learning disability, the psychologist should work with a special education teacher to make sure that the child receives the educational services that will help him best compensate for his learning difficulties.

Can parents help in the comprehensive evaluation?

They certainly can. Parents possess important information that they need to share with the experts, for parents know their child better than anyone else. The professional should be asking the parents many questions in trying to understand the child's day-to-day behavior and activities and to get as clear a picture of the child as possible. Indeed, one of the hallmarks of a good ADHD assessment is the inclusion of a number of standardized questionnaires for parents to complete about their child.

Should I expect my child's school to provide an evaluation if I request one?

The Individuals with Disabilities Education Act (IDEA), which has replaced the Education of the Handicapped Act, provides for the evaluation of, and appropriate special education for, students with disabilities. However, to be eligible for special education services, the student must meet the eligibility requirements stated in this law. ADHD is not currently listed in the law as one of the categories that make children eligible for these services. Consequently, many schools tell parents of children with ADHD that their children are not entitled to special services and that the school cannot help them. Other schools try to fit children with ADHD into one of two other eligibility categories under the IDEA: "learning disabled" or "other health impaired." However, this strategy does not work for many children with ADHD. In fact, there are so many children with ADHD not being served properly that the United States Congress is currently studying whether to amend the law to add ADHD as an eligibility category. Another federal statute, Section 504 of the Rehabilitation Act, does provide coverage for students with ADHD if their impairment substantially limits their ability to learn. Section 504 provides for evaluation and special education services, just like the IDEA, but most school districts are unfamiliar with Section 504. The bottom line, then, is that parents of children with ADHD may need to contact their local support group for help in getting appropriate services from their school district. A listing of some of the major national support networks for parents of children with ADHD is contained in Appendix A.

Does it matter how old my child is when an evaluation is performed?

Children of all ages can be evaluated for ADHD, although more evaluation options are available for older children because they are more verbal and can comprehend more complex testing instructions. Many of the tests currently available require certain basic verbal and thinking skills that only an older child would be likely to possess. So, for children younger than 5 or 6, an evaluation for ADHD usually consists mostly of behavioral observations in different situations rather than formal testing.

How do children feel when they find out they have ADHD?

Many children are confused upon learning they have ADHD. Some think that there is something terribly wrong with their bodies or their brains, and some even think that they might die. Some might use this diagnosis as an excuse to behave even more poorly, saying, "I can't help myself—I have ADHD!" Others, however, will be relieved because finally someone understands why they have so much trouble paying attention at school, following rules, and obeying their parents. Most of these children *want* to behave well, and they find it troubling to have so much difficulty doing so. For them it is less a matter of "I won't behave well" than "I can't behave well"—or, at least, "I find it very difficult to behave well."

How may parents feel about their child's having ADHD?

Children with ADHD are not the only ones who experience a wide range of feelings. Some parents, when first told that their child has ADHD, experience a feeling of denial. They tell themselves, "No, this is not true . . . it is not happening to my child . . . my child cannot possibly have ADHD . . . you must be wrong." Some parents even become angry and criticize the classroom teacher for failing to provide adequate instruction or for having a negative attitude toward their child. Some parents become worried or even fearful, asking, "What is going to happen to my child? Is she going to lead a terrible and unhappy life?" Many parents also experience guilt, thinking they must have done something wrong to cause the ADHD or should have done something to prevent it. And finally, many parents feel sad and helpless because they are unsure how best to help their child.

But many parents also feel relief upon hearing the diagnosis of ADHD. The parents have lived with the child all of her life and undoubtedly know that something is "wrong"—that this child is not like the other children in the neighborhood or even the other children in the family. Once an accurate diagnosis is made, it at least explains *why* this child is different. After all, parents cannot begin to solve the problem before they know what the problem is.

How may siblings feel about having a brother or sister with ADHD?

Siblings of children with ADHD also experience many different and sometimes confusing feelings. They may wonder if they are to blame for their brother's or sister's problems. They may even wonder whether they will "catch" the ADHD or whether their sibling will die from the disorder. They may not understand why their brother or sister gets so much of their parents' attention or gets punished so often. Because of all their unanswered questions, they too may feel angry, frustrated, afraid, and/or guilty. Parents are advised to sit down with the brothers and sisters of a child with ADHD, as well as with the affected child, and explain the situation to them in language they can understand.

How can I explain my child's behavior to other family members and people in the community?

With other children, such as siblings or peers, your child's behavior may be explained in the following manner: "All children are born different. They are born with different hair colors, different eye colors, and different sizes. Children are even born with different abilities to do certain things. Some children can run faster than others, some can play games like baseball more easily than others, and some can learn to read or do math problems more quickly than others. Some children even find it easier to pay attention, to be patient when they are trying to do something, or to stay in one place for a long time. Unfortunately, some children have problems paying attention and have trouble taking their time and sitting still when they are trying to do something. These children sometimes have problems finishing their schoolwork, getting along with other children, and doing what parents and teachers ask. It is important that we help these children so that they can be happier and less frustrated."

Is there anything else I can say to adults who are involved with my child in order to help them understand his behavior?

It is not uncommon for adults involved with a child who has ADHD to make comments about the child's inappropriate behavior. These adults may include teachers, principals, people within religious institutions, scout leaders, coaches, and grandparents and other relatives. It would be in your child's best interest to explain about ADHD to adults who are actively involved in his life. This will help them understand that he is not necessarily misbehaving deliberately to anger them.

An adult can understand that everyone's brain works differently: For example, in some people's brains, the vision area operates in such a way as to require eyeglasses. And in the brain of a child with ADHD, certain areas (usually the front parts) are not stimulated enough to enable the child to pay close attention to boring or uninteresting tasks, to think about the consequences of actions before acting, or to sit still for long periods. Like the person who compensates for poor vision by wearing eyeglasses, the child with ADHD needs to receive special support services and compassionate understanding to compensate for his problems. You can let concerned adults know that there are a number of treatments for ADHD that are being considered for your child and that some of these treatments will likely help both in and outside of the home—to decrease behavioral difficulties, to increase his feelings of success in performing activities and in getting along with others, and thereby to increase his self-esteem.

What can I, as a parent, do to help my child if she does have ADHD?

In addition to the treatment options that will be discussed in later chapters, it is vital that a child with ADHD be provided with as many success-oriented experiences as possible. She should have opportunities to interact with same-age peers in noncompetitive activities that minimize failure. Although the child with ADHD should be encouraged to attempt challenging activities, she should not be forced continually to engage in activities that are extremely frustrating. Identify your child's strengths and interests, and encourage participation in activities that call on her strengths and appeal to her interests. For instance, a child with ADHD who is particularly skilled at drawing should be encouraged to pursue art activities.

Specific ways for parents to help their child feel good about appropriate behavior will be discussed in later chapters. If a child can be made to feel successful through a variety of experiences, she will likely come to feel that she can truly have a positive impact upon her environment. Children who have high self-esteem and who believe they can exert a positive influence often are more motivated to try new things and to establish healthy relationships with others.

CHAPTER TWO

Treatments for Attention Deficit Hyperactivity Disorder

Once a child has been appropriately diagnosed as possessing ADHD, one or more treatments may be attempted. A number of treatments and techniques have been found useful in helping children with ADHD, and we will discuss these throughout the book. Although most research suggests that a combination of treatments is most effective, it is important to understand that no treatment approach is thought to "cure" ADHD. Rather, with the right combination of treatments, the frequency, intensity, and duration of problems associated with ADHD may be reduced.

What treatments are available to help the child with ADHD?

The most common treatment for ADHD is, and has been for some time, psychostimulant medication. There are many types of such medication; the most commonly used is methylphenidate, often referred to by one of its trade names—Ritalin. Other psychostimulant medications include *d*-amphetamine (or Dexedrine) and pemoline (or Cylert). Such medication is thought to exert its beneficial effects by stimulating the brain areas that enable a child to sustain attention, delay impulsive responses, control motor activity, and plan behavior.

Since caffeine is a stimulant, can I just give my child coffee, tea, or cola instead of psychostimulant medication?

Most studies that have examined the effects of caffeine on children with ADHD have found little positive support for the use of caffeine in ADHD treatment. Caffeine taken by these children has often been found either to be ineffective or to be less effective than psychostimulants. Therefore, caffeine is not considered very useful in alleviating the symptoms of ADHD.

Is it true that psychostimulant medications are mind-altering drugs?

The answer is yes, but only in terms of activating the attention, body movement, organization, motivation, and planning ability centers of the brain. Psychostimulants are definitely *not* mind-altering drugs in terms of changing one's personality or one's perception of reality. In other words, although psychostimulant medications may help a child to better focus his attention, delay impulsive responding, and organize himself in a more efficient manner, they do not cause him to experience distortions of reality.

If these medications are stimulants, why do they seem to calm children with ADHD?

Although the medications frequently given to children with ADHD are psychostimulants, they do not increase the child's activity level. Indeed, because these medications appear to have a calming effect on such children, some have called their effects paradoxical. However, in reality there is nothing paradoxical about the effects of psychostimulants on children with ADHD. This becomes clear when one recognizes that the psychostimulants primarily affect the areas of the brain that support focused attention, planning, and organization. When the child with ADHD becomes better able to focus her attention and plan her behavior, she will appear less distractible, less impulsive, and less disorganized. All of these changes will result in a decreased activity level—after all, if she is glancing around the room less, is better able to resist impulses to get out of her seat, and is more organized in her efforts, she will be less physically active than if she is looking around, moving about, and behaving randomly. In fact, recent studies have shown that children without ADHD are affected in exactly the same way by psychostimulants as are children with ADHD. That is, children without ADHD are also better able to focus attention and organize behavior when on small doses of psychostimulants.

Are you saying that my child will be fine once he takes the medication?

The answer is maybe. In a comprehensive literature review conducted by Barkley (1977), it was concluded that only about 75 percent of children with ADHD taking psychostimulant medication are judged significantly improved, whereas about 25 percent do not improve or are made worse by the medication. In addition, although such medications have been shown to have short-term effects such as increased attention span and decreased impulsiveness, little change has been found with respect to the social, academic, or psychological adjustment of children with ADHD as they grow older. It appears that the psychostimulant medications are helpful for temporary control of ADHD symptoms but may not be helpful in the long run. In other words, psychostimulant medication seems to be effective for the immediate management of children with ADHD, but it may not be helpful in preventing future social and academic difficulties. One reason that the medication may not enhance future adjustment is that taking medication does not teach a child any skills; it only helps him to pay attention, as well as to control and plan behavior.

How do I know whether medication is the right treatment for my child?

After your child has received a comprehensive evaluation and been diagnosed as having ADHD, she may be referred to a physician to determine the appropriateness of the use of psychostimulant medication. Remember, only a physician, such as your child's pediatrician, can decide whether your child should be placed on psychostimulant medication. If so, the physician will ultimately be responsible for managing the medication treatment. Medication is generally not prescribed for children under the age of 6, as its safety and effectiveness for such young children have not been well established. If medication is recommended, the physician should first give it on a trial basis to determine whether it is helpful and, if so, what the proper dosage is.

How exactly does the physician conduct this trial?

One popular means for conducting this trial is a *double-blind, placebo-controlled study*. By using this method, a physician can evaluate impartially whether psychostimulant medication is an appropriate treatment for a child with ADHD. The procedures used in this kind of study are somewhat complicated and should be directed by the physician prescribing the medication, often with the aid of a psychologist. Most physicians typically do not perform double-blind, placebo-controlled studies because they are time consuming and require specialized knowledge. For this reason it is often helpful to have a knowledgeable psychologist involved—to help ease the time demands on the physician and to help coordinate and implement the procedures.

In a double-blind, placebo-controlled study the child with ADHD is given the psychostimulant medication on some days, whereas on other days she receives a placebo, a pill containing no medication at all. The child, her parents, and her teachers will not know on a given day whether the medication or the placebo is being taken; only the physician (and psychologist, if one is involved) will have this information. Both the parents and the teachers then make daily ratings of the child's behavior. In addition to these behavioral ratings, certain psychological tests, which measure attention span and impulsivity, can be used to monitor the effectiveness of the medication. If the medication is helpful, the daily behavior ratings and the psychological tests will show improvement primarily on the days the child takes the psychostimulant medication, as opposed to the placebo. If the medication is not helping the child, either there will be no improvement regardless of the type of pill she takes or there will be an equal amount of improvement when she takes the medication and when she takes the placebo. The physician may also use different medication dosages in a double-blind fashion to determine the most appropriate dosage for a particular child. A double-blind, placebo-controlled study is useful in evaluating the effects of psychostimulant medications because psychostimulants show immediate effects, unlike certain other medications that show their effects only after some time has elapsed.

If my child shows improvement while taking the placebo, should the placebo then be considered an appropriate treatment?

It is not recommended that children receive a placebo as a treatment for ADHD. One of the most important reasons for this is that some children begin to attribute improvement in their behavior to the pill rather than to themselves. Because a placebo cannot alter the brain centers involving attention, impulsiveness, motor activity, or planning and organizational ability, it is best to teach children that they can control their own behavior rather than relying on a pill for that control. With children who do receive medication regularly, it is very important to stress that their improved ability to complete tasks and control their behavior is due to the fact that they want to do so and are doing so themselves. They need to be convinced that the medication only helps them to pay attention and control themselves a little better—that the medication is not magic and doesn't do the work for them. Sometimes it is important to impress this upon teachers and others as well!

What are the side effects of psychostimulant medication?

The most common side effects of psychostimulant medication are decreased appetite and insomnia. These two side effects are clearly understandable when one remembers that these medications are stimulants. Many coffee drinkers pass up that beverage close to bedtime, as it can easily cause difficulty in falling asleep. For the same reason, a child with ADHD given psychostimulant medication shortly before bedtime may have increased difficulty falling asleep. In addition, stimulants tend to decrease appetite; indeed, most diet pills are simply some form of stimulant, usually caffeine. Consequently, it should not be surprising that psychostimulants can also cause some children to be less hungry than they might be when not on medication. Less common side effects include irritability, headaches, stomach pain, and excessive sadness or crying.

Can side effects be eliminated, or will my child have them for the rest of his life?

Fortunately, the side effects of psychostimulant medication, such as those just mentioned, are usually dose dependent. This means that the severity of the side effects often depends on the dosage of the medication—the higher the dose, the more severe the side effects. Thus, the physician can often decrease the severity of unwanted side effects simply by decreasing the dosage of the medication. If adequate relief from side effects cannot be obtained with

a lowered dose of medication, then the medication should
be removed altogether.

I've heard that these medications often lead to drug addiction or interfere with a child's growth—is this true?

There are a number of misconceptions regarding other side
effects of psychostimulant medication. One concerns an increased potential for drug abuse. However, research has
suggested that children who receive such medication are no
more likely than other children to become addicted to or
dependent on street drugs when they are older. In fact, it
has been suggested that children who have taken stimulant
medication for ADHD may be less likely to use other drugs
when they are older: Many of them seem to have greatly
disliked taking medication as children, and they may be
more aware of the importance of appropriate and safe
medication use.

Another misconception is that stimulant medication greatly
suppresses skeletal growth and weight gain. Children who
receive high doses of such medication do have an increased
risk of height and weight suppression, but this usually
occurs during the first year of treatment. Such children
typically make up for delayed growth soon after this first
year of treatment, experiencing little or no impact upon
adult height and weight. Nevertheless, to help minimize
any possible interference with growth, many physicians
prefer to remove children from medication when they are
not in school—during summer months, over holidays, and
sometimes on weekends.

Can the medication make children "crazy" when they are older?

There has been much recent debate about whether medications such as Ritalin cause future emotional or behavioral
difficulties. Research has not substantiated such harmful
future effects, although harmful effects have been reported
in some cases when medication was administered in excessive doses over long periods or when medication was prescribed to children who should not have been receiving it.
For instance, highly anxious children or those with muscular
tics may not be particularly good candidates: Psychostimulant medication has been shown to be less useful with such

children, and in some cases it may even aggravate their anxiety or muscular tics. Some also believe that children with seizure disorders or epilepsy should not be prescribed psychostimulants because such medications may increase seizure activity. Another indicator against the use of psychostimulant medication is the presence of certain mental disorders such as thought disturbances. In addition, psychostimulants can interfere with the activity of other medications; other medications, such as antihistamines, can also alter the effectiveness of psychostimulants. Be sure that your child's physician carefully rules out these indicators before prescribing any medication.

Should my child's medication treatment be monitored regularly?

Yes. The physician should be kept informed of any side effects, as well as observable benefits, that you think your child is experiencing. In addition to your regular reports, the physician can use a double-blind, placebo-controlled study to monitor the effects of the medication about every 12 months. Such reevaluations are necessary because a child's attentional and self-control abilities may improve over time. Such improvement may lessen the need for continued psychostimulant treatment. Also, as children mature, they gain weight. Because the effects of psychostimulants are, to some extent, influenced by body weight, adjustments in the medication dosage may be needed as your child becomes heavier.

How do I help my child avoid feeling embarrassed or angry at having to take medication at school?

Some children become embarrassed or angry because schoolmates tease them about having to take special medicine. It is important to work out a daily dispensing schedule with the school nurse to ensure that your child receives the medication. To avoid scrutiny by other children, your child might plan to visit the nurse during times that are least noticeable, such as right after lunch and before going to the playground. However, the best way to help a child feel less embarrassed, angry, or just plain different from others is to make sure that other children understand your child's disorder and the need for medication. You can help educate your child's teacher and, in turn, you can both educate your child's schoolmates. You might also suggest ways for your child to tell friends about ADHD and its treatment. (You may want to refer to chapter 1 for suggestions on how to do this.)

Is it true that psychostimulant medication is not helpful for teenagers and adults?

There is no specific age at which such medication becomes ineffective. Some people continue to take the medication into adolescence and even adulthood and find that it continues to be beneficial. Others, on reaching adolescence or adulthood, discontinue medication because they no longer find it beneficial or because their problems are no longer severe enough to justify continued medication use. Again, continual and close monitoring of the medication, including periodic reevaluations, is highly recommended.

What treatments other than medication are available for children with ADHD?

A second treatment for children with ADHD is cognitive-behavioral self-control therapy, or CBT. CBT is based on the idea that children develop self-control as a result of language development. The behavior of very young children is controlled by the language of others—especially their parents. That is, parents tell their very young children what to do and what not to do. For example, when a 1-year-old crawls toward an electrical outlet, the parent says, "No, no, no . . . don't touch." As the child grows older, however, it is expected that she will become better able to control her own behavior without constant parental supervision. The child is now expected to tell herself not to touch the electrical outlet.

People who support CBT believe that some children, and especially children with ADHD, have increased difficulty learning to use language for self-control. These children consequently need extra coaching in using language to control their own behavior. Basically, that is what CBT tries to do—teach children to talk to themselves as a way of controlling their own behavior.

What kinds of techniques are used in CBT?

A number of training methods are used in CBT to teach children with ADHD to better control themselves and solve problems more effectively. The first step in most CBT training programs is to teach the child to recognize when he is having a problem and to stop his actions until he has had time to think about the problem and about how he will try to solve it. One common delaying technique is to take a deep breath and think, "Stay calm . . . get relaxed." The next step typically is to teach the child to examine the problem situation—that is, to think about what caused the problem and to set a goal identifying how he wants things to turn out. In the third step, the child is taught to come up with as many different possible solutions to the problem as he can think of and then to evaluate each possible solution. Finally, the child is taught to pick the best solution from all those he has thought of and to try out that solution to see how well it works.

Can you give me an example of how a child would use such techniques during a problem situation?

Let's suppose that a boy named Chuck has problems getting along with other children on the school playground. His CBT would focus on helping him solve problems more effectively and delay his impulsiveness toward other children when he goes to the playground. During CBT, Chuck's therapist can teach him problem-solving strategies and self-control skills and can set up role-plays—simulations of probable playground events—to let Chuck practice what he has learned. In role-playing, Chuck and his therapist can act out problematic events that are likely to occur outside the therapy setting.

Perhaps an example of Chuck's CBT would be useful here: Chuck's problem is hitting other children in response to teasing on the playground. Chuck's therapist teaches him several strategies. He is taught first to identify his problem by becoming aware of his *thoughts* (such as "That boy is really making me mad . . . I'm going to slap him!"), his *feelings* (such as angry, sad, scared, and unhappy), and his *behaviors* (such as tense muscles, clenched fists or teeth, crying, upset stomach, and headache). When Chuck realizes he has a problem, he needs to take a deep breath and tell himself, "Stay calm . . . get relaxed." Next Chuck needs to think about what caused his problem and decide on a goal for the way he would like things to turn out. In this case, his problem is that another boy teased him, and his goal is to stop being teased by that boy. Chuck's therapist encourages him to come up with several possible solutions to his problem and to evaluate these solutions. In this situation, Chuck's solutions might include hitting the other boy, telling the playground supervisor, saying nothing and walking away, and teasing the other boy. Chuck is taught to evaluate his solutions in a variety of ways. For instance, he could ask himself whether a solution is safe, how it might make other people feel, and what might happen next if he chooses that particular solution.

Chuck reflects that if he hits the other boy, both of them might get hurt and they would probably be sent to the principal's office or maybe even be suspended from school. If Chuck tells the playground supervisor, then the other boy might get in trouble and might not bother him again; on the other hand, the boy might get very angry at Chuck for tattling and might decide to continue the teasing. If Chuck consistently walks away from the other boy and ignores the teasing, then the other boy might get tired of not getting a reaction and might decide that teasing Chuck is no longer fun. If Chuck teases the other boy, then the other boy might get angry and hit Chuck or decide to tease him even more.

After contemplating his four solutions, Chuck finally decides that the best one is to walk away from the other boy while ignoring the teasing. Chuck will try that solution out and see how well it works. Regardless of whether or not the chosen solution actually works, he will give himself a pat on the back by telling himself, "Good job! I'm using my problem-solving plan!" If his solution does not work out as well as he had hoped, the therapist will encourage him to try some of his other solutions or think of new ones.

How well does CBT work?

Although CBT used by itself can be helpful in some cases, it has not proven to be a particularly effective treatment for ADHD when used alone or when used with children younger than 4 or 5. Thus, CBT is most effective in combination with other treatments, such as medication or instruction in specialized parenting techniques, and with older children. In fact, with respect to age, it is our experience that CBT is best understood by, and most helpful with, children between the ages of 7 and 11.

The bibliography and reference list at the end of this book suggests additional readings about cognitive-behavioral or self-control therapy. Because CBT requires a great deal of specialized training, we will not attempt to describe its specifics further. For more information about this treatment approach, it is best to contact a licensed mental health professional.

What other treatments besides medication and CBT are available for children with ADHD?

After medication, the most common treatment for ADHD consists of specialized techniques that parents can learn for managing their child's behavior. Parenting is one of the most important yet most difficult and frustrating jobs in the world. After all, children do not come equipped with a set of instructions. The job is even more difficult for parents who must face the numerous behavior problems associated with ADHD. Parents are often forced to do the best they can under the circumstances; unfortunately, what they try may not always work. Therefore, parents often need to learn specialized techniques and strategies to help their children become more successful in meeting their responsibilities and getting along with others.

What sort of specialized techniques do I need as a parent to help my child with ADHD be more successful?

Parents can learn several important techniques that have proven to be effective in helping children with ADHD. Among these are behavioral charting, "Very Special Time," use of positive reinforcers and negative consequences, behavior contracts, and daily home report cards. These specialized techniques, when used together, can enable a parent to teach the child with ADHD more appropriate ways of behaving by communicating love, warmth, and concern within a context of firm limit setting. The rest of this book will describe these and other specialized parenting techniques in more detail.

CHAPTER THREE

Observing Behavior: The Technique of Charting

In order for children with ADHD to learn appropriate self-control behaviors, parental discipline must be consistent and systematic. Children with ADHD require much structure and clearly defined expectations and limits. If consistent management and structure are lacking, these children will be quite confused about the behaviors that are expected from them. This chapter will present one technique, called *charting*, for increasing consistency and structure in the home.

What is charting?

Charting is the first step in any behavior change program. It requires that parents very specifically define the behavior that is the focus of concern so that it can be observed and counted. If you cannot actually count the instances of the behavior you want to change, then you have not specified it clearly enough. For instance, saying that a child is disobedient can mean many things. It can indicate that the child does not follow parents' requests, does not complete school homework, or does not complete household chores. Saying that a child is cruel or aggressive may mean that the child frequently swears, hits, yells at others, or breaks things. The idea behind charting is to specify the behavior you want to change so precisely that you can actually count the number of times it occurs.

Why is it so important first to chart a behavior before trying to change it?

Charting is an important first step in any behavior change program for several reasons. First, charting allows parents to find out how frequently a particular behavior is occurring.

This information is important because it will help you decide whether or not a behavior really needs to be changed. Indeed, some behaviors are so bothersome that they appear to occur more often than they actually do. For example, it may seem as though your child *never* obeys your commands, but when you actually chart how often she does so, you may discover that she really is obeying 80 percent of the time. Consequently, her disobedience may be less of a problem than you had originally suspected. Or you may think your child and her sister *never* get along, but charting reveals that most of the time they get along quite well—it's just that when they do fight it is very disturbing to you. Charting can reveal just how difficult some of your child's behaviors really are and which troublesome behaviors are most in need of change.

A second reason why charting is an important basis for any behavior change program is that careful observation can make parents more aware of their own behavior. This increased self-awareness can give parents clues about how to change their children's behavior. For example, parents whose child throws frequent temper tantrums may come to realize through charting that they almost always eventually give in to the child's temper outburst. Or parents whose child does not obey their requests may discover that the child is often allowed to get away with noncompliance when she starts to cry. Charting, then, by allowing parents also to observe their own behavior, may reveal how they may unintentionally be encouraging some negative behavior in their child.

A third reason why charting is so important is that careful observation can make the child more aware of a particular problem behavior. For example, your child may not notice how often she ignores your commands or whines when asked to do something. In fact, a decrease in inappropriate behavior and a corresponding increase in appropriate behavior is sometimes seen when parents simply record the occurrence of behaviors in a calm and consistent manner.

Is charting used only before a behavior change program has begun, or does it continue even after the program is under way?

You should continue charting even after a particular behavior change program has begun because it can help you determine the effectiveness of your actions. Charting takes the guesswork out of evaluating your efforts—it provides specific information about whether your child's problem behavior is decreasing and whether the appropriate behavior is increasing. Information gathered from charting is particularly important because most behavior change comes slowly to children with ADHD and may be difficult to notice. And when a behavior change program is not working, charting can provide clues about what might be going wrong.

How do you record behaviors during charting?

There are a number of ways to record behaviors during charting. First, you can record the *frequency* of a behavior. This means recording how often a behavior occurs—for example, how often your child leaves his toys in the living room or hits his brother. Second, you can record the *duration* of a behavior, noting how long a behavior lasts—for example, how long it takes your child to get ready for bed at night or to finish a household chore. Third, you can record a *ratio* of appropriate to inappropriate behaviors. For example, you can record both the number of times your child obeys your commands and the total number of commands you give him. You can then calculate your child's compliance rate by dividing the number of times your child obeys by the total number of commands (for example, one child may obey 3 of 6 commands for a 50 percent compliance rate, whereas another might obey 4 of 20 commands for a 20 percent compliance rate).

Once you have chosen the best way to record a particular behavior, you can begin to record this behavior on a behavioral chart. The chart should be as simple as possible so that both you and your child can easily see what is being recorded. If there are two parents in the home, both should be equally involved in charting. For example, the parents could count and record the same behavior at different times of the day, or they could count and record different behaviors during the same times.

It is very important that parents count and record both the inappropriate behavior they want to decrease and an appropriate substitute behavior. For example, if you want to decrease disobedience, you should chart both the number of times your child does not obey your commands and the number of times he does obey.

Must I count and record my child's behaviors all day long?

If the behaviors to be recorded occur very often, you can determine their overall frequency by recording just 1 or 2 hours each day. However, if the behaviors occur infrequently, it may be necessary to count and record them throughout the day. A general rule of thumb is that if the behavior occurs fewer than five times a day, it should be counted all day long. If it occurs five or more times a day, it can be counted over a shorter period—whatever period is required for the behavior to take place at least five times. However, no matter how frequently the behavior occurs, under no circumstances should you count and record the behavior for less than a half hour. Another hint is that if there are certain situations when the inappropriate behavior is especially likely to occur, charting may only need to be done during those times. For example, some children are especially disturbing during mealtimes or when you are on the phone. In such a case, it may suffice to chart the behavior only then.

What happens when we are away from home? Do I still need to chart then?

It depends upon the behavior. However, most children with ADHD do have some behavior problems outside, as well as inside, the home. If this is true for your child, then you will also need to chart behavior when your child is outside the home. An easy way to do this is to carry a small notepad or index card when you leave home and simply make a tally mark whenever the behavior occurs. Another strategy for charting behavior outside the home is to put a coin in one pocket whenever the misbehavior occurs and a coin in another pocket whenever the more appropriate behavior occurs. Later you can count the coins in each pocket and record those numbers on the behavior chart.

What should I tell my child about charting?

Always explain to your child why you are charting. For instance, you might say, "One of the problems we want to work on at home is having you do what we ask without arguing. So we are going to count how often you argue with

us when we ask you to do something, and how often you
do not argue with us when we ask you to do something."

Where should these charts be kept?

It is best to keep the behavior charts in a visible spot, perhaps on the refrigerator door or on a kitchen cabinet. And
remember, it is important to keep these charts as simple as
possible so that they are readily understandable.

Can you give me some examples of charting?

We have many examples of successful charts from the hundreds
of families with whom we have worked. Following are three
examples from our case files; they illustrate different ways of
charting behavior.

CASE EXAMPLE 1 _____

Frequency of Behavior

Teddy is an 8-year-old boy who continually causes problems
at home by hitting his sister, Lorri. This behavior leads to
much screaming and yelling, and Lorri often runs crying to
her parents to complain about Teddy's hitting. The parents
are extremely irritated by this constant unpleasantness. In
order to determine how often Teddy is really hitting Lorri,
the parents decide to chart Teddy's behavior for a week.
However, the parents want to know not only how often
Teddy is hitting his sister but also how often he is able to
play nicely with her. Before charting Teddy's behavior the
parents explain to him, "One of the problems in our home
is your hitting Lorri. We would like you not to hit Lorri.
Instead we would rather see you playing nicely with her.
So, we are going to count how many times you hit Lorri and
how many times you play nicely with her."

As you can see in Figure 1, Teddy played nicely with Lorri an
average of 1.7 times per day; this average is the number of
times that Teddy played nicely with his sister during the entire
week (12) divided by the number of days in the week (7). Teddy
hit his sister an average of three times per day; this average
is the number of times that Teddy hit Lorri during the entire
week (21) divided by the number of days in the week (7).

Figure 1 Sample Frequency Chart

Name _____ Teddy _____   Week of _____ March 17 _____

Appropriate behavior	Sunday	Monday	Tuesday	Wednesday	Thursday	Friday	Saturday
Playing nicely with sister	I	IIII	II	I		III	I
Total appropriate behaviors	1	4	2	1	0	3	1

Weekly average of appropriate behavior = _12_ (total frequency) ÷ _7_ (number of days) = _1.7_ times per day.

Inappropriate behavior	Sunday	Monday	Tuesday	Wednesday	Thursday	Friday	Saturday
Hitting sister	IIII	II	III	HHT I	III		III
Total inappropriate behaviors	4	2	3	6	3	0	3

Weekly average of inappropriate behavior = _21_ (total frequency) ÷ _7_ (number of days) = _3_ times per day.

In a situation like Teddy and Lorri's, parents also have the option of charting the behavior of both the child with ADHD and the sibling if each seems to be contributing to the fighting. That is, a single chart can be developed for both children so that when fighting occurs, regardless of who started it, that behavior can be recorded.

CASE EXAMPLE 2 _____

Duration of Behavior

Cindy is a 9-year-old girl who seems always to be late for her school bus. Cindy's parents have observed that what delays her the most each morning is her inability to get dressed quickly enough. The parents decide that if Cindy is able to reduce the time that she spends getting dressed, they won't have to resort to waking her up earlier and she may be able to catch the bus on time. To determine just how long it takes Cindy to get dressed, her parents decide to chart the time that elapses from the ringing of their daughter's alarm clock until the time she is dressed. They explain to Cindy, "One of the problems we want to work on at home is that you seem to be late for your school bus a lot because you are taking a long time to get dressed in the morning. We would like to see you get dressed as quickly as possible after your alarm clock rings. So, we are going to time you to see how long it takes you to get dressed each school day."

As Figure 2 shows, it takes Cindy an average of 46.8 minutes to get dressed each morning; the parents obtained this average by adding the total number of minutes it took Cindy to get dressed during the entire week (234 minutes) and dividing it by the number of school days in the week (5).

CASE EXAMPLE 3 _____

Ratio of Appropriate to Inappropriate Behavior

Barry is a 7-year-old boy who does not appear to mind his parents very well. His parents are extremely frustrated by his failure to follow their instructions or do what they ask him to do. Often, out of frustration, they eventually end up yelling at him and sending him to his room; this not only provides Barry with some attention from his parents but

Figure 2 Sample Duration Chart

Name ___Cindy___ Week of ___September 10___

Behavior	Sunday	Monday	Tuesday	Wednesday	Thursday	Friday	Saturday
Minutes it takes Cindy to get dressed in the morning from the time her alarm clock rings	(not recorded/ not a school day)	62 minutes	37 minutes	53 minutes	43 minutes	39 minutes	(not recorded/ not a school day)

Weekly average = ___234___ (total minutes) ÷ ___5___ (number of days) = ___46.8___ average number of minutes per day.

also enables him to avoid obeying their requests. Barry's parents devise a chart to find out just how much of the time Barry does obey their requests. They chart not only the number of times during each day he obeys their requests but also the number of times he does not comply. The parents explain to Barry, "Things don't always go as well at home as we would like. And one of the problems that we need to solve is your not doing what we ask you to do. So, we are going to mark down the number of times you do what we ask you to do and the number of times that you do not do what we ask you to do."

As Figure 3 shows, Barry's parents calculated a daily compliance rate and a weekly compliance rate for their son. To obtain the daily rate, they added the number of times that Barry obeyed their requests during that day and divided the sum by the total number of requests for the day. For the weekly rate, they added the number of times Barry obeyed requests during the entire week and divided the sum by the total number of requests for the entire week. By charting this behavior, Barry's parents learned that he obeyed their requests 50 percent of the time during the past week.

Numerical information like that shown on the sample charts in Figures 1 through 3 will be useful to you as you attempt to modify your child's behavior. In chapter 5, we will discuss this subject in more detail. The next chapter details a technique for changing the cycle of negative interaction that can often arise between parents and their children with ADHD.

Figure 3 Sample Ratio Chart

Name ___Barry___   Week of ___January 3___

	Sunday	Monday	Tuesday	Wednesday	Thursday	Friday	Saturday
Appropriate behavior *Does what we ask*	I	II	IIII		̶I̶I̶I̶I̶ I	III	I
Total appropriate behaviors	1	2	4	0	5	3	1
Inappropriate behavior *Does not do what we ask*	III	IIII	IIII	II	II	I	
Total inappropriate behaviors	3	4	4	2	2	1	0
Daily percentage (appropriate behaviors per day ÷ total behaviors per day)	1/4 = 25%	2/6 = 33%	4/8 = 50%	0/2 = 0%	5/7 = 71%	3/4 = 75%	1/1 = 100%

Weekly compliance ratio = ___16/32___ (total appropriate behaviors ÷ total behaviors recorded) = ___50___ %.

CHAPTER FOUR

Very Special Time

Frequently, parents and their children with ADHD develop a habit of interacting in very negative ways: The child seems to be constantly misbehaving, and as a consequence of this misbehavior the parents find themselves becoming very critical and negative toward their child. It is very important to break this cycle of negative interaction. One specialized parenting technique for changing this negative pattern is called *Very Special Time.*

What is Very Special Time?

Very Special Time is based on an agreement that, for 10 or 15 minutes each day, you will give your child your complete and undivided attention and allow him to be the boss. During that time your child may choose what to do or play—so long as he follows three simple rules. First, your child may not choose to do anything that is harmful to himself or to anyone else. So, no hitting during Very Special Time. Second, he may not do anything that is destructive to property. So, no jumping on the furniture! And third, Very Special Time must take place in the home (or, in nice weather, in the yard). So, no shopping expeditions. As long as your child follows these three rules, you must agree to do whatever he wants to do during these 10 or 15 minutes.

Very Special Time is quite different from simply spending time that is special with your child. For example, a trip to the movies may be an enjoyable time together, and it may be very special, but it is *not* Very Special Time. What distinguishes Very Special Time is that your child is the boss. At all other times when you are together, *you* are the boss.

How do I go about setting up this Very Special Time?

First, choose the time of day that you want to offer Very Special Time to your child. It is very important that *you*

43

determine the time of day. Your child decides *what* to do during Very Special Time, but you decide *when*.

Is there a time of the day that is best for Very Special Time?

The best time varies from family to family. Some families like to offer Very Special Time in the evening. For others, the best time is just after school. We've even known some families who have set aside time in the morning, before school. At first you can experiment with different times to find out what works for your family, but eventually it is best to make Very Special Time a part of your daily routine. It might always occur right after dinner, or right after bath time, or just prior to preparations for bed. If Very Special Time becomes part of your daily routine, it is unlikely that you will forget it (after all, most of us don't forget other daily activities, such as eating dinner). In time your child will stop questioning you about when he will have Very Special Time that day; he will know when to expect it.

And remember, during Very Special Time your child should have your complete and undivided attention. So, don't try to combine it with cooking dinner or preparing the children for bed. In fact, it is important to communicate to your child that nothing except a real emergency will interrupt your Very Special Time together. Thus, if someone calls on the phone for you during this time, arrange to return the call later.

What if I can't always guarantee that I can give Very Special Time at a particular time each day?

Although it is best to work Very Special Time into your daily routine, the life-styles of some families make this unrealistic. One alternative is to make a Very Special Time Clock, a clock with movable hands and a written notice on top stating: "Very Special Time will be given today at: _____." Each morning you can move the hands of the clock to indicate when Very Special Time will take place that day.

What should I do after I decide when to offer Very Special Time?

Talk with your child in advance about Very Special Time. Tell him that during this time, he will be the boss and can decide what to do. Explain that as long as he follows the three rules mentioned earlier, you will agree to do whatever he wants to do during Very Special Time. It is crucial to emphasize that, although your child is the boss for these 10 to 15 minutes each day, *you* are the boss the rest of the day. Although you must do what your child wants to do during Very Special Time, the rest of the day he must do what you say.

Once you tell your child about Very Special Time, it is very important that you actually offer it consistently. One of the potential benefits of this approach is that, eventually, your child will learn to count on your complete and undivided attention for these 10 to 15 minutes each day and will not feel the need to pester you for attention at inopportune times.

You keep mentioning that Very Special Time should be about 10 to 15 minutes long. Is this time frame exact, or can the time be longer than that?

Generally, Very Special Time can last either 10 or 15 minutes each day. It does not seem to be very effective if offered for less than 10 minutes; it may even be harmful if it lasts longer than 15 minutes because no child should be the boss of his parents for more than a quarter of an hour each day. Look realistically at your family schedule and decide whether you can manage 10 or 15 minutes each day for Very Special Time.

Once you have decided on the duration, you should use a timer to signal the beginning and end of Very Special Time. The timer is very important. When it sounds after 10 or 15 minutes, Very Special Time must be ended *immediately.* Do not allow your child to manipulate you into prolonging it. No matter how much screaming or pleading your child does, Very Special Time must end when the timer goes off. You can always spend other time together in other activities, but your child can be the boss for only 10 or 15 minutes. For the rest of the day, *you* are the boss.

What do I do if I cannot offer Very Special Time once in a while?

There certainly will be times when it is impossible for you to offer Very Special Time to your child, and he will simply have to accept this when it happens. However, if these "emergencies" start happening more often than not, you may need to reevaluate your commitment to the approach. In fact, if you cannot commit to offering Very Special Time on a consistent basis, it is better not to do it at all.

If I miss Very Special Time one day, can I make it up the next day by doubling the time?

Definitely not! If you start doing this, pretty soon you will wind up owing your child hours of Very Special Time.

How do I begin Very Special Time each day?

It is best to give a 5-minute notice that Very Special Time is about to begin. Simply approach your child and say, "Very Special Time will begin in about 5 minutes. So think about what you'd like to do today during your Very Special Time, and I'll be back in 5 minutes." This will give your child some time to organize himself for what he wants to do and to finish any activities already in progress.

In about 5 minutes, go back to your child and say, "OK, Very Special Time has started. What would you like to do today?" Then start the timer for either 10 or 15 minutes. If your child still has not decided what to do during this time, say that he can spend some of the Very Special Time talking with you about things you could do together. But under no circumstances should your child's indecision about which activity to engage in be used to delay the start of Very Special Time.

What do I do during Very Special Time?

Above all, let your child decide what to do; let him control the action. Your job is to be *with* your child and to *attend to whatever he is doing*. Relax and have fun. This is a time when you can forget about being a parent for a while and just enjoy being with your child.

You should also avoid asking questions or giving commands. You may find this very difficult because most parents interact with their children primarily through questions and commands. However, questions are intrusive, and commands only serve to provoke confrontations during Very Special Time. Commands should be used only if your child's behavior becomes inappropriate—that is, if he breaks one of the three rules stated earlier.

If I can't give directions or ask questions during Very Special Time, what can I do?

Instead of commands and questions, use *active listening*. Basically, this involves describing what your child is doing. One method is to pretend you are a sportscaster and describe what you see going on. For example, if your child wants to play checkers with you during Very Special Time, you might say, "So you would like to play checkers tonight . . . Now you are getting out the checkerboard . . . and now you are placing the checkers on the checkerboard." You may feel uncomfortable at first, but eventually both of you will come to enjoy this way of interacting.

Occasionally, you can give *positive feedback* about how much you are enjoying being with your child. This is not necessarily praise, but rather a positive statement concerning what you like about your time together. You might say, for example, "I like it when you and I play quietly together" or "I like it when you and I can sit down and have a nice conversation together." Your comments should generally express what you like about what your child is doing. Try to avoid using the type of praise that focuses on inappropriate behavior: For instance, it is better to use the preceding statements than to say, "It's nice not to argue with you for a change" or "I like it when you don't throw your toys around the room." Comments that point out how your child is *not* misbehaving only serve to remind him how he *could be* misbehaving.

What should I do if my child misbehaves during Very Special Time?

First, it is important to remember that misbehavior during Very Special Time is defined *only* as breaking one of the three rules mentioned earlier in this chapter. Any other inappropriate behavior displayed during this time should be ignored. So, for example, if your child screams and yells during Very Special Time, you should ignore it. However, if the screaming is so loud or so close to your ear that it is causing real pain (as opposed to merely annoying you), it would be in violation of the rule that your child cannot do anything during Very Special Time to hurt himself or anyone else.

If your child does break one of the rules, first point out that he is breaking a rule and that if he continues to do so, you will stop Very Special Time for that day. Then, if he continues to break the rule, *calmly* leave the room. Do *not* say things like "I'm trying so hard to be nice, but you always mess things up!" (Later in the book we will discuss ways to deal with misbehavior when it occurs at other times of the day.)

Should my other children be involved in Very Special Time as well?

No other children should be involved in this Very Special Time unless your child specifically requests that the others also participate. And please resist the temptation to try to persuade your child to let siblings join in. This is *his* Very Special Time, and no matter what he chooses to do (so long as it is within the rules), you should try not to judge the choice of activity or quality of play.

Should I offer a separate Very Special Time to my other children?

If you have more than one child at home, you can do one of two things: You can give Very Special Time to each child, or, if this is not feasible, you can explain to your other children that Very Special Time is a new strategy you are trying so that things will go better at home not only for the child with ADHD, but for the whole family as well.

If I don't offer Very Special Time to my other children, won't they be upset?

Rarely does giving Very Special Time only to the child with ADHD result in an increase in misbehavior by siblings. This is because the other children already know how to interact appropriately with their parents and already get ample attention for positive behavior. However, parents do sometimes make the mistake of unintentionally beginning to ignore their other children as they become more involved in a positive way with the child who has ADHD. That is another reason for limiting Very Special Time to 10 or 15 minutes—so that you can also spend time with your other children, although perhaps in a less structured way.

Should Very Special Time be offered by the parents together or separately?

Very Special Time should be offered by one parent at a time—*not* both at the same time. If there are two parents in the home, both need to be actively involved in order to increase the likelihood of positive behavior change. Two parents can offer Very Special Time to the child on alternate days, or each parent can offer it separately each day. It is not desirable to leave Very Special Time to one parent if both are living in the home.

How long will I have to continue offering Very Special Time?

Ideally, Very Special Time should continue indefinitely. However, at a minimum you should offer it consistently for 6 months to 1 year to give it a fair chance to work.

Is there any age limit for the usefulness of Very Special Time?

Generally, there is no lower age limit for using Very Special Time. It has even been used successfully with infants and toddlers. However, some older children may find the approach somewhat babyish. Although there is no hard-and-fast upper age limit for the appropriateness of Very Special Time, most children will enjoy it until they become teenagers. However, even some teenagers find this shared time enjoyable, so let your child be your guide in this. If he clearly is turned off by the idea, then let it go. But if his face lights up with enthusiasm at the idea of being the boss, you know he still wants to have Very Special Time!

Can a parent overdo Very Special Time?

Absolutely! There are two ways that a parent can overdo Very Special Time. The first is to allow the special rules of this time to become the household rules. Some parents, that is, start to believe they should always interact with their child as they do during Very Special Time. This is a sure way to make your child's behavior worse, not better! Your child should not be the boss except during these special 10 or 15 minutes.

At all other times, even when the two of you are doing something enjoyable together, you need to be the boss.

A second way a parent can overdo Very Special Time is by using it as an excuse not to do other things with the child. Your child needs your attention and involvement for more than just 10 or 15 minutes each day. In the next chapter we will look at other ways besides Very Special Time to attend to your child's positive behavior.

CHAPTER FIVE

Increasing Appropriate Behavior

Increasing appropriate behavior is a very powerful way of managing the misbehavior of children with ADHD. As a child's positive behavior increases, negative behavior must decrease; after all, a child cannot both behave and misbehave at exactly the same time. The use of techniques for encouraging positive behavior as a means of managing misbehavior also has the advantage of teaching appropriate behavior. Punishment, by contrast, only teaches a child how not to behave. This chapter will focus on ways to increase your child's appropriate behavior through the use of *positive reinforcement* techniques. In chapters 6 and 7, we will talk more about the setting of limits and the use of discipline in the home.

How can parents increase their children's positive behaviors?

One way for parents to increase the frequency of their children's positive behaviors is through positive reinforcement. According to this principle, if a person is rewarded after a certain behavior, then it becomes more likely that the person will repeat that behavior. In other words, if a parent pays attention to a child's behavior or otherwise rewards it, it is more likely that the behavior will occur again. However, if the parent ignores the behavior or withholds a reward, it is less likely that the behavior will be repeated. For example, if your child makes her bed in the morning and you pay attention to this fact—either by praising her or by providing some kind of reward or positive reinforcer—it becomes more likely that she will make her bed the next morning. If, on the other hand, you ignore her having made the bed or punish the behavior by criticizing the quality of her bedmaking, then the probability decreases that she will make the bed in the future.

51

awesome example

Unfortunately, positive reinforcement works whether it follows good behavior or misbehavior. Thus, if you buy your child candy following a temper tantrum in the supermarket, you increase the likelihood that she will throw another tantrum the next time she wants candy. She has learned that temper tantrums work; they get her what she wants—in this case, candy. And all the scolding in the world after you get home will not undo her learning that temper tantrums work.

The trick with positive reinforcement, then, is to become very skilled at attending to your child's positive behavior while ignoring her misbehavior as much as possible (although, as we will discuss in later chapters, there will be times when parents cannot ignore misbehavior and must provide discipline). Indeed, one of the biggest mistakes most parents make is thinking that it is important to pay attention to their children no matter what. Paying attention is important, but parents must be selective in knowing when to pay attention. Moreover, positive attention will be most effective if you learn to use your attention consistently to reinforce good behavior. To accomplish this, you should pay lots of attention to your child when she is behaving well and ignore her as much as possible when she is misbehaving.

→Important Statement

Keyword

↓ Important Opinion Statement (strong)

What are some examples of positive reinforcers? ★

There are several kinds of positive reinforcers. First, there are *social reinforcers*, such as smiles, hugs, verbal praise, pats on the shoulder, kisses, and so on. A second type is *material reinforcers*; these are things like special desserts, stickers, money, toys, records, and books. A third type of reinforcer includes *activities that your child enjoys*, such as going on a family outing, playing a table game with the family, watching television, or playing catch. Finally, *extra privileges*, such as using the parents' stereo or their special work tools, staying up late, or using the family car, can serve as reinforcers. The general rule of thumb is that anything your child enjoys can serve as a positive reinforcer.

It could be as simple as rewording your phrases. Instead of "Johnny, if u don't eat your food you will not be able to play w/ your cars."

How do I use activities as positive reinforcers? ★

Using preferred activities as positive reinforcers can be a powerful method for increasing appropriate behavior. What

You could say, "Johnny, you can play w/ your cars when you get done eating"

this entails is allowing your child to engage in a pleasurable activity, such as playing Nintendo or going bike riding, only after he performs some less pleasurable activity, such as doing homework or cleaning up his bedroom. Psychologists have a fancy name for this—the Premack Principle. But most grandmothers will tell you that they used this principle long before some psychologist gave it a name. Again, the basic idea is that *first* your child does something you want, and *then* he gets to do something he wants to do. For instance, *first* your child does his homework, and *then* he watches TV. (It won't work to allow him to watch TV first and then try to get him to do his homework.)

Imp.

Why must I reward positive behavior? Shouldn't my child want to behave well without being rewarded for it? ✶

refer to p. 62 about bribery

It would be nice if children just naturally wanted to behave well. But the reality is that children must learn correct behavior, and it is the parents' responsibility to teach them how to behave well. Just hoping or expecting that your child will naturally behave well will only lead to a great deal of frustration for you and your child alike. ✶ refer to p. 63

I've tried paying attention to my child when she is doing something good, and all it seems to do is get her riled up. Why does this happen, and what should I do about it?

For children who have had lots of practice behaving poorly, it can happen that when their parents first start to pay attention to them for good behavior, they are stirred up to misbehave. This is because, for some children, the most effective way to capture and keep their parents' attention is to behave poorly. Consequently, when parents start to pay attention to the child for good behavior, the child may automatically begin to misbehave out of habit. Unfortunately, if parents avoid paying attention to good behavior out of fear that it will incite misbehavior instead, it becomes less likely that the child will repeat the appropriate behavior that was ignored.

How do I go about starting to pay more attention to my child's good behavior?

One helpful way to increase the amount of time you spend paying attention to good behavior is to begin to *catch your child's good behavior.* This means watching for times when your child is behaving well and then giving him some kind of positive reinforcement. For instance, when you ask your child to do something and he obeys your request, you should immediately provide social reinforcement in the form of positive feedback, explaining how much you like it when he does what you ask the very first time. You might say, "Thank you so much for doing what I asked" or "I like it when you do as I say" or "It's wonderful when you do as I ask." If you just walk away from your child after he obeys your request, you have essentially ignored that behavior and made it less likely that he will comply with your instructions in the future. (Remember: Behavior that is ignored is generally less likely to be repeated.)

It is also important to avoid using compliments that are criticisms in disguise. Examples of such back-handed compliments are "Will wonders never cease! You did what I asked!" and "Why can't you be this good all the time?" Such comments will only cancel out the positive attention you are trying to show to your child.

What if my child completes a task without my telling her to do so?

If you discover that your child has completed a chore or followed a household rule without being told to do so, you should pay special attention to this to encourage her to comply spontaneously again. You could say, "Wow! That's fantastic! You're feeding the dog all by yourself!" or "You really are growing up! You made your bed without Dad or I having to remind you or tell you to do it!" Extra attention paid to your child at these times will increase the probability that she will complete such tasks again without direct parental instruction; she will have learned that following home rules without reminders earns very special positive attention from her parents.

What if one of my children obeys a request but my other child does not?

If one of your children has gotten into the habit of disobeying your instructions, be sure to pay more attention to the children who do obey than to the child who misbehaves or requires reminders. This teaches all your children that, to receive positive attention from you, they must obey your instructions. Of course, you should be especially careful also to pay attention to your more difficult child whenever she does obey your instructions. The point here is that parents have a very powerful tool in the use of positive attention to acknowledge obedient behavior and in the withholding of positive attention from disobedient behavior.

Would charting be useful in catching my child's good behavior?

Yes! As a matter of fact, a very good method for reminding yourself to attend to your child's appropriate behavior is to use a form of positive reinforcement that we call a Catch Your Child's Good Behavior Star Chart. The purpose is to further increase the impact of your attention to appropriate behavior by also placing a star on a chart for every time you catch your child behaving well.

What does this star chart look like?

An example of such a star chart is shown in Figure 4. As you can see, the chart has a separate space for each day of the week, with stars posted on the days that the child earns them. Before using the chart, be sure first to sit down with your child and explain that you will be trying to catch his good behavior—and that when you do, you will say so and put a star on the chart. Thereafter, when you notice your child engaging in a desired behavior, say something like "Fantastic! I just caught your good behavior! I'm going to go put a star on your star chart!" and add a star for that day. Try to catch your child's good behavior as much as possible, ideally at least five to eight times per day. The chart should be placed in a conspicuous spot, where it can both remind your child to behave well and remind you to catch his good behavior.

If I start giving stars, won't my child start demanding them in order to behave appropriately?

This will become a problem only if you begin to award stars when your child demands them. It is important, in explaining the star chart to your child, to emphasize that it is your job to catch his good behavior—and that you cannot do this if he points out his own good behavior or demands a star in

Figure 4   Sample Catch Your Child's Good Behavior Star Chart

Name   _Johnny_   Week of   _May 20_

Sunday	★ ★ ★ ★ ★
Monday	★ ★ ★ ★
Tuesday	★ ★ ★ ★ ★ ★ ★
Wednesday	★ ★ ★ ★ ★ ★ ★ ★ ★
Thursday	★ ★ ★ ★
Friday	★ ★ ★ ★ ★ ★
Saturday	★ ★ ★ ★ ★ ★ ★

advance of it. Thereafter, if your child nags you or tells you that he has been good and deserves a star, simply repeat that only you can catch his good behavior.

[handwritten margin note: be firm + consistent]

Do I just give my child a star for any good behavior, or can I single out a specific behavior to work on?

[handwritten margin note: I am just going to give this one example of a star chart, because there are more examples + I have copies of them to pass out.]

At first it is useful to use the star chart to reward lots of different kinds of good behavior so that your child will begin to get the idea that you will be paying attention to it. However, after a while you will probably want to start to single out specific behaviors to work on. Whenever you do decide to single out specific behaviors, it is important to let your child know in advance what behaviors will earn stars. You might say, for example, that you will be watching for times when he does what you ask the very first time without a fuss, or that you will be giving him stars for playing nicely with his sister or for engaging in any other positive behavior that you would like to see more often.

When you use a star chart to reward a single, specific behavior, it is often helpful to set a goal—a behavioral achievement toward which your child can work. But before you can set a goal for your child, you first have to find out to what extent he is already performing the positive behavior you want to increase; this is called a *baseline*. You obtain a baseline by charting for one week the specific behavior you want to increase, as illustrated in chapter 3. For this baseline week, you would not pay any more attention to the behavior you are charting than you normally would. For example, if the desired behavior is obeying your commands, you should first chart how often your child is already complying without paying special attention to that behavior.

Once you have this baseline, you can decide on an appropriate goal for your child to work toward. In setting a goal, it is critical not to require too great an improvement over the baseline. Rather, the emphasis needs to be on rewarding small, but positive, improvements in your child's behavior. The weekly goal should be raised only 5 to 10 percent per week, even if your child far surpasses the goal during any given week. Raising goals only a small amount each week helps keep your child from becoming overly frustrated by increased demands for progress.

Can you give an example of how this might work?

Suppose, for example, that Natalie's parents want her to better follow the family rule of turning off the TV set when leaving the TV room. The first step would be to determine how much of the time she is already obeying this household rule. Natalie's parents therefore first charted her behavior for 1 week, using a ratio chart like the one Barry's parents used to chart Barry's compliance with their requests (see Figure 3 in chapter 3). This baseline charting indicated that, during the week, Natalie obeyed the rule 10 times but failed to obey it 20 times; that is, on 20 different occasions she left the room without turning off the TV. This gave a compliance ratio of 33 percent (10 compliances divided by 30 requests). Natalie's parents then set her weekly compliance goal at a level just slightly above this baseline, say at 35 percent.

Natalie's parents knew that stars tend to be more rewarding than tally marks, so once the weekly goal was established, they began using stars to indicate the number of times she remembered to turn off the TV. To determine the number of times she remembered, they simply counted the stars as if they were tally marks. At the same time, however, they continued to use tally marks to record the number of times she did not turn off the TV set when leaving the TV room. Figure 5 illustrates how the stars were used and how Natalie did on the second week of the program.

Because Natalie exceeded her goal of 35 percent compliance, at the end of that week her parents could provide her with a special reward—perhaps a small toy or a trip to a fast-food restaurant. The following week, the goal could be raised *provided Natalie had reached her goal the week before.* For instance, the next week she might be required to follow the TV rule 40 percent of the time in order to earn a weekly reward. This process would continue until she was obeying the household rule at some acceptable level. At that point, her parents might want to stop focusing on that particular behavior and begin to work on another problem behavior.

Can I use stars if I'm interested in changing the duration of a behavior?

Yes, you can. If you recall, Cindy was the girl described in chapter 3 who had trouble catching the schoolbus. Her

Figure 5 Sample Star Chart for Specific Behaviors

Name _____Natalie_____   Week of _____June 3_____

	Sunday	Monday	Tuesday	Wednesday	Thursday	Friday	Saturday
Appropriate behavior *Turning TV off when leaving room*	★	★	★		★★	★★	★
Total appropriate behaviors	1	1	1	0	2	2	1
Inappropriate behavior *Leaving TV on when leaving room*		/		///	//	/	///
Total inappropriate behaviors	0	1	0	3	2	1	3
Daily percentage **(appropriate behaviors per day** **÷ total behaviors per day)**	1/1 = 100%	1/2 = 50%	1/1 = 100%	0/3 = 0%	2/4 = 50%	2/3 = 67%	1/4 = 25%

Weekly compliance ratio = __8/18__ (total appropriate behaviors ÷ total behaviors recorded) = __44__ %.

parents might put a star on her duration chart (see Figure 2) for each day she gets up and out the door on time.

When you do use stars to indicate appropriate duration of a behavior (such as the amount of time it takes to get dressed in the morning or the amount of time spent getting ready for bed at night), be sure to continue the duration recording as well so that you can keep track of whether your child is achieving her weekly behavioral goal. It is also important to remember that when you use a duration chart, you will need to give positive reinforcement either for reductions in the time your child spends engaged in an inappropriate behavior or for increases in the time your child spends engaged in an appropriate behavior. So, your child might earn rewards for decreasing the time it takes her to wash the dishes or for increasing the time she spends helping the family work on the backyard garden.

If I begin to work on a specific behavior, should I stop using the more general Catch Your Child's Good Behavior Star Chart?

It is usually a good idea to continue to pay attention to other good behavior in addition to the specific behavior you have decided to work on. This can be done in one of two ways. First, you can continue to keep a separate chart for catching your child's other good behavior. Then whenever you catch your child doing something good other than the specific behavior you are working on, you can reward him with a star on the more general star chart. A second method is to use only one chart, but use a different color star to reward your child's behavior if it is not the specific behavior you are working on. You can call these bonus stars or extra special stars. By continuing to reward other good behavior in addition to the specific behavior you are working on, your child will continue to try to behave appropriately in a variety of different ways.

What if the behavior I'm working on involves a sibling as well as my child with ADHD?

If you are working on a behavior change program concerning both the child with ADHD and a sibling, you can use the same methods to set goals for rewards. Recall, for instance, the example of Teddy and Lorri's fighting, described in chapter 3. Their parents could use the baseline information on fighting frequency to set a weekly goal. If, as shown in Figure 1, the weekly baseline of "nice play" is 1.7 times per day, then a weekly average goal of about 2.0 times per day of "nice play" would be reasonable. If both children meet that goal by the end of the week, both should receive the weekly reward for which they were working. Of course, the parents would then slightly raise the weekly goal required for the next week's reward. When charting is used both for the child with ADHD and for siblings, it is recommended that weekly rewards entail something positive that the children can enjoy together, such as playing in the park or joining in a special game. It is hoped that such joint rewards will help encourage positive interaction between siblings.

What should I do if my child does not reach the weekly goal?

If your child does not reach the goal for a particular week, simply keep the same goal until he is able to reach it. Lowering the goal may be necessary if your child repeatedly falls short of it. As mentioned earlier, it is very important to avoid demanding too great an improvement from week to week; otherwise, your child is apt to become discouraged and give up.

How do I decide on the reward my child should work for?

The reward can be anything from a small toy to a family outing. The best way to determine a good reward is to ask your child what he would like to earn. You then can decide which of his ideas are reasonable given the family budget and your availability. To keep the reinforcers surprising from week to week, some families prefer to write several ideas on slips of paper and put them in a container. After the child has reached his goal for the week, he draws one of the slips of paper to determine what his reward will be. Of course, whenever you use material reinforcers and special privileges and activities as rewards, do not forget to provide lots of verbal praise as well.

Should I be setting only weekly goals for my child?

It is often good to set both daily and weekly goals. For example, if you are working on increasing the amount of homework your child does each night, the daily goal might be to complete at least 15 minutes of homework, and the weekly goal might be to complete at least 2 hours of homework over the entire week. Smaller, daily rewards can be given when your child reaches his daily goal, and larger, weekly rewards can be used for rewarding the attainment of the weekly goal. The daily rewards should be relatively modest (for example, a quarter, a pencil or pen, a small pad of paper, or extra stay-up time at night); weekly rewards can be more significant (for example, a trip to McDonald's or a videotape rental of your child's choice).

I'm having trouble with the idea of giving my child things for behaving himself. Isn't that bribery? refer to p. 53

Parents sometimes feel a bit uncomfortable using positive reinforcement techniques because they think they are bribing their child to behave. If we look at the most common definition of the word *bribery*, however, we will see that it means offering or giving something to someone in order to persuade that person to act dishonestly. In contrast, positive reinforcement consists of providing material or nonmaterial rewards (or incentives) *after an appropriate behavior* in order to increase the likelihood that the child will display even more appropriate behavior.

Parents also sometimes worry that if they start giving rewards for appropriate behavior, their child will start to demand rewards before doing anything appropriate. This will not happen, however, if the parent always waits until the appropriate behavior has occurred to offer a reward. No child should be allowed to demand that the parent promise a reward for appropriate behavior. As a matter of fact, such a demand should be ignored or even met with a disciplinary action, such as a 5-minute time-out (to be discussed in chapter 7).

refer to p. 55

How quickly will my child's behavior improve when I use these reinforcement techniques?

The use of positive attention and rewards tends to improve behavior very slowly. It is unlikely that you will see dramatic improvements in a short time. In fact, you might even find an initial increase in misbehavior when you first start using reward programs. Remember, your child with ADHD has spent years developing the habit of misbehavior, and it will take some time to help him develop the habit of appropriate behavior. So don't expect positive changes overnight. But if you persist at catching his good behavior and using star charts, in the long run your child's behavior *will* improve.

How long will I have to continue catching my child's good behavior and using star charts?

In the beginning, it will be important to catch your child's good behavior very frequently. In fact, the use of material rewards along with verbal praise will probably be necessary whenever you begin concentrating on a particular appropriate behavior. However, once you start to notice that your child is engaging in the behavior more and more often, you can reinforce him for that behavior less frequently. Indeed, once your child begins to display an acceptable level of the appropriate behavior, you may want to stop focusing on that behavior and begin working on another behavior instead.

Do children learn only from rewards?

Absolutely not! Besides learning from rewards, children also learn from *negative reinforcement*. What this term means is that a person is likely to repeat any behavior that stops an unpleasant situation. For instance, if you pester your child to do her chores, she may finally do the chores as a way of putting an end to your pestering. This is the problem with nagging your child—eventually it may work! And if it does, you will be more likely to nag her again in the future. Now, unless you really like to nag, this situation is generally unpleasant for everyone. It is far more desirable to teach your child to do the chores at the first request by using positive reinforcement techniques.

Another example of negative reinforcement is demonstrated by the child who throws a temper tantrum when asked to do something that she does not want to do. If you give up and don't enforce your command when a tantrum occurs, then your child will have learned that throwing a temper tantrum is an effective way to turn off your commands. Therefore, every time you give your child a command, it is very important for you to follow through and make sure that she obeys—especially if she has developed the habit of tantruming whenever she is asked to do something she does not want to do.

Don't children also learn from observing other people?

Others certainly do serve as *models* for how children should behave. In fact, modeling and observation are the most important means for learning new behaviors (whereas positive reinforcement, such as rewards and incentives, is most important for increasing the frequency of appropriate behaviors or for maintaining a particular appropriate behavior at a level that pleases parents). Furthermore, children often use their parents' behavior as a model for their own, rather than listening to what their parents say about how they should behave. Generally, for instance, children who see their parents smoke, but are told not to smoke themselves, are more likely to become smokers. And parents who advise their children not to swear, but who frequently swear themselves when they are angry, are really teaching their children that swearing is the way to deal with frustration or anger.

On the other hand, modeling can be a powerful tool for teaching children desirable behaviors. Children can learn responsibility by watching their parents do household chores without complaining, neatness by watching their parents hang up their clothes after they have taken them off, table manners by watching their parents display appropriate eating habits, and sharing by watching their parents share materials such as tools, games, books, or records. They can learn the skill of compromise by watching their parents allow other family members to choose the TV program or activity for an evening. The point is that children learn by watching others; if you want your child to behave in certain ways, try to behave in those ways yourself as much as possible.

CHAPTER SIX

Decreasing Inappropriate Behavior

Thus far, we have only discussed ways of increasing your child's appropriate behavior, techniques that are very important in teaching and encouraging your child to behave well. However, you may need other techniques to help your child learn how *not* to behave. That is, you will also need to know how to respond to misbehavior. Indeed, part of your parenting job is to provide structured limits for your child with ADHD so he can learn that it is important to listen to others and follow rules. Those two skills will eventually become quite important for your child as he learns to interact with others in the social and work aspects of life. This chapter will present some initial ideas on how to manage your child's misbehavior.

In other words

Setting limits

Conclusion

our job as care takers

How can parents decrease inappropriate behavior?

transition to 2nd factor

As mentioned earlier, parents can increase the frequency of their child's appropriate behavior by paying attention to it or rewarding it. In fact, paying attention to appropriate behavior will cause some decrease in misbehavior as well because a child cannot engage in both appropriate and inappropriate behavior at exactly the same time. However, simply paying attention to appropriate behavior will not eliminate all misbehavior.

A simple first step in trying to decrease the frequency of your child's inappropriate behavior is to *ignore* it. This may work because misbehavior is sometimes simply a way to get attention: The payoff for the misbehavior is increased attention from the parents. If this is the case, ignoring misbehavior should decrease its frequency because the child is no longer getting the payoff—that is, the child no longer gets the parents' attention by misbehaving.

How do I go about using ignoring as a way to decrease my child's misbehavior? ✶ - reply

A first step is to observe and chart how often your child's misbehavior occurs and how often you pay attention to it when it does occur. If your charting indicates that your child is often successful at getting your attention by doing inappropriate things, you might try ignoring the misbehavior as much as possible while attempting to catch your child's good behavior. This method is difficult, however, because most parents respond much more frequently and consistently to inappropriate behavior than to appropriate behavior. And this parental response may teach children that misbehaving is the quickest and most effective way to get their parents' attention.

Sum up phrase

You should be aware of one possible problem in the use of ignoring for decreasing misbehavior. The problem is that, when you first start ignoring your child's misbehavior, the frequency of the misbehavior may actually increase, not decrease. This may occur because your child is used to getting your attention through misbehavior, and when you suddenly stop attending to it, her first response may be to "turn up the volume." It is as if the child is saying, "Hey, wait a minute! Didn't you see me misbehave? In case you didn't notice, here is the misbehavior again!"

very important summary

If you choose to use ignoring, it is very important not to give up too quickly. It is also important to use a star chart and make a real effort to catch your child's good behavior. This way, your child will quickly learn a different way of getting your attention, one that does not involve misbehavior.

Should all misbehavior be ignored? ✶

Certainly not! There are some misbehaviors that should not be ignored. For example, dangerous behaviors such as mishandling sharp tools, playing with matches, and carelessly crossing a busy street should not be ignored because of the potential injury that could result. Other behaviors that should not be ignored include stealing and vandalism, as well as certain refusal behaviors, such as disobeying parental instructions or failing to complete household chores. If parents ignore their child's unwillingness to do such things as clean his bedroom, set the dinner table, or water the yard, the child will learn that refusing his parents' instructions is an easy way to evade chores or obligations.

How should I deal with misbehavior that cannot be ignored?

There are several additional ways of dealing with the misbehavior of your child with ADHD. The first of these relies on what we call *natural consequences*. From this method, which is really only a slight variation on the ignoring technique, the child learns by experiencing the naturally occurring unpleasant consequences of an inappropriate behavior. When using this technique, parents should look for situations in which misbehavior will lead to a naturally occurring unpleasant consequence for the child. Then parents should ignore the misbehavior so that the child can learn for herself what happens if she engages in it. This procedure also helps a child develop responsibility for herself and learn to foresee possible negative consequences of her own behavior.

As an example, suppose your child breaks or loses one of her toys because she played with it too harshly or left it out in the rain. If you ignore this inappropriate behavior by not buying a replacement toy, your child will have learned that she should take better care of her toys. Likewise, if she comes home late after the family dinner hour because she was playing with a friend and lost track of time, then she may miss dinner that evening. Of course, natural consequences should not be used if they are dangerous to the child, to others, or to the property of others.

Are there other types of consequences besides natural consequences that I can use when my child misbehaves?

As a matter of fact, parents can respond to misbehavior with several other types of consequences, called *logical consequences*. That is, when the child behaves inappropriately, the parents give an unpleasant consequence that is logically tied to the misbehavior. This technique should be used when the naturally occurring unpleasant consequences for a particular misbehavior are either nonexistent or not very powerful.

What are some examples of logical consequences?

One type of logical consequence is called *response cost*. It involves removing a positive reinforcer, such as a desired object or activity, following inappropriate behavior. In other words, there is a cost to the child for behaving inappropriately. For instance, if the child forgets to turn off the TV set when he is done watching a program, then he may lose TV privileges for the next day or two: The cost for not turning off the TV is losing viewing privileges. If a child typically misbehaves at the store, the parents may choose to leave him at home on the next shopping day. The cost for misbehaving at the store is being excluded from the next shopping trip. In another approach to the shopping situation, the parents might tell the child upon arriving at the store that he may spend some money (for example, 50 cents) at the end of the shopping trip if he behaves well, but that each time he misbehaves 5 cents will be deducted from the original amount. The cost of misbehavior here is 5 cents per instance.

A second type of logical consequence is called *overcorrection*. It involves having the child improve things over the way they were before the inappropriate behavior occurred. In other words, the child will need to overcompensate or overcorrect for his own misbehavior. As an example, if a child leaves a mess in one area of the family living room, then he may be required to clean up the entire room in addition to tidying up his own mess. The same principle applies to a child who purposely breaks or steals something: He would be required to replace more than just the broken or stolen item. For instance, if a child deliberately broke one of his sister's records, he might be required to replace the broken record and buy her another one as well. And if he stole a dollar from his mother, he would have to repay her 2 dollars.

A third type of logical consequence, called *positive practice*, involves having the child practice an appropriate way of behaving after he has behaved inappropriately. This method helps educate a child about the expected behavior as well as discipline him for the misbehavior itself. Take the example of a child who has trouble scraping and rinsing his own dishes after each meal. The child may be required not only to clean his own dishes but also to take care of the entire family's dishes for 1 or 2 days. This technique can be used for a variety of behaviors. Let's say that a young child often runs into the street without looking both ways to check for oncoming traffic. He may be asked to practice the right way 5 to 10 times under strict parental supervision.

How do I go about administering a logical consequence?

When you first notice your child misbehaving, calmly but firmly inform her what consequence will occur if she chooses to continue to misbehave. You might say, "If you choose to continue playing your music too loudly, then your radio will be taken away for a day." If she decides not to turn down the radio, it is crucial that you carry out the logical consequence. You can then let your child know that the following day she will have another chance to behave appropriately when it comes to playing the radio in the house.

Why haven't you mentioned spanking as a way to decrease my child's misbehavior?

We stress alternatives to physical punishment, both because physical punishment tends to be much less effective than the other techniques we have talked about and because it is usually unpleasant for both children and parents. Physical punishment, such as spanking, may also have some undesired side effects. For instance, a child who is frequently spanked by his parents may eventually come to avoid them because he fears a spanking. As a result, the parents would have fewer opportunities to be with their child and to teach him more appropriate behaviors. Physical punishment can also cause emotional difficulties such as fear, worry, intense sadness, or increased disobedience in children. The child who receives frequent physical punishment may even become more physically aggressive toward others because his parents are inadvertently teaching him that the way to deal with problem situations is through physical aggression.

What do I do if my child refuses to obey the logical consequence or if I can't think of a good logical consequence?

In the next chapter we will talk about another way of providing discipline in addition to the use of natural and logical consequences. This technique, called time-out, can be used to cope with a variety of inappropriate behaviors.

CHAPTER SEVEN

Time-Out

Time-out is a technique that can be quite useful in dealing with misbehavior, especially with younger children. Time-out involves removing a child from a pleasant situation in response to a misbehavior and then placing him in a less pleasant situation. Time-out is especially useful when ignoring a particular misbehavior might be viewed by the child as beneficial. For instance, if you ignore your child's refusal to perform a household chore, you may actually be rewarding the disobedient behavior; the child will have gotten away with noncompliance. Time-out is also an effective alternative to spanking and other forms of physical punishment, which tend to be upsetting and unpleasant for everyone involved— including parents!

What exactly is time-out?

Time-out is a variation on having a child sit in the corner or some other designated place for a specific time after he has misbehaved. The idea behind the technique is that, when your child is not in time-out, he has the opportunity to be involved with people in positive ways and to engage in enjoyable activities—for example, earning stars for his star chart or receiving praise from you. When in time-out, however, the child is ignored for a specific period. Not only does he receive no praise or other positive reinforcement, but he receives virtually no attention at all. You should even refrain from scolding the child who is in time-out, as scolding is itself a form of attention.

Where should the child be during time-out?

The time-out spot should be a dull and boring place where your child will not have access to enjoyable, rewarding, or interesting activities. It should not be a place where things like books, toys, TV, radio, or even other people's attention are easily available. It is advisable to choose a place without breakable objects nearby, just in case your child becomes very upset or agitated while in time-out. A dull corner in a hallway will often satisfy these requirements; many families find that the bottom step of a staircase is a useful time-out spot as well. If you do use a chair in a corner as your time-out spot, place the chair far enough from the wall so that your child cannot kick at or hit the wall.

The time-out spot should *not* be a dark or frightening place. For example, a closet, attic, or other small space should definitely not be used for time-out—this could inadvertently teach your child to fear small or dark places. Your child's bedroom is also not a good time-out spot because it usually contains lots of interesting things to do. Similarly, the bathroom is not very useful, because your child might spend the time playing in the sink or finding entertainment in the contents of drawers or cabinets.

How old should a child be before I can use time-out?

Time-out is most useful with younger children. Generally, children as young as 3 can both understand and learn from the technique. It becomes less useful with older children, and it generally should not be used with children older than 10. In fact, using time-out with older children can actually make their problems worse!

How do I go about using time-out in my home?

As with all of the other parenting techniques we have talked about, you should first sit down with your child and calmly explain how you will be using time-out. This discussion will be much more effective if you choose a neutral time. That is, don't try to explain time-out procedures while your child is having a temper tantrum or misbehaving in some other way.

Your explanation should stress that time-out will be used *every time* the child engages in a certain misbehavior—that particular misbehavior will always result in a time-out. If the child refrains from the misbehavior, there will be no time-out. Remember that you should also be positively attending to some appropriate behavior that can replace the misbehavior—for example, by adding stars to your child's star chart. Thus, it is important to remind your child of ways to earn your positive attention instead of time-outs. For example, he can choose to earn stars for doing what you ask the very first time, or he can earn time-outs for disobeying you. He can earn stars for playing nicely with his sister, or he can earn time-outs for hitting or teasing her. He can earn stars for picking up after himself or time-outs for leaving things around the house. Emphasize that it is your child's choice—to earn a reward by behaving appropriately or a time-out for misbehaving.

How might I actually explain time-out to my child?

You might explain time-out in this way: "I know that sometimes you have trouble doing what I tell you to do the very first time without a fuss (or any other misbehavior you want to decrease, such as hitting, swearing, whining, teasing, and so on). From now on, whenever you don't do what I ask the very first time, I will repeat what I want you to do, and I'll warn you that if you don't do it this time, you will go into a time-out. If you get the warning and you don't *immediately* do what I have asked, you will then have to take a time-out. This means you will have to sit in a time-out chair in a corner of the hallway. After you have gone to the time-out chair and are absolutely quiet, I will start a timer. When the timer rings you can come out of time-out if you have sat quietly the whole time. Don't forget that we're also using the star chart for doing what I ask the very first time without a fuss. So if you do what I ask the very first time without a fuss, not only will you not get a time-out, but I will also try to catch your good behavior and put a star on your star chart."

When I use time-out, must I always give a warning?

It depends on the behavior you are trying to change. For example, if you are trying to decrease your child's disobedience, it is often useful to give a time-out warning if he does not obey your first command. However, there are other behaviors for which a warning is less appropriate. If, for instance, the problem behavior is hitting other people, it is reasonable to tell your child in advance that whenever he hits someone, you will *immediately* send him to time-out. "No hitting" thus becomes a household rule; the warning consists of your explanation to your child that he will receive a time-out any time he breaks this rule. Similarly, if you are trying to decrease swearing, a warning is not needed. As a rule, if you want your child to *start* some behavior, such as obeying your commands, a warning should be given. If you want him to *stop* some behavior, such as hitting, swearing, or teasing, you do not need to give a warning.

How long should my child spend in time-out?

Generally, research has shown that small negative consequences given consistently are much more effective in reducing the frequency of misbehavior than are large negative consequences given inconsistently. Therefore, time-out need not last very long. Usually 5 minutes of time-out suffices for children between the ages of 3 and 10. In other words, 5 minutes of time-out tends to be just as effective for a 4-year-old as for a 9-year-old. You should use a timer or an alarm wristwatch to keep track of your child's time-out period.

Although the time-out may be short, it is very important that it be *continuous quiet time.* Do not start the timer until your child is sitting absolutely quiet in the time-out spot. If the child starts to talk, whine, yell, or scream after the 5 minutes has started, simply reset the timer.

You should also emphasize to your child that only parents determine when a time-out is over, and not the child or his siblings. Thus, your child must wait for your OK to leave time-out, as well as for the timer's signal.

What should I do if my child refuses to go to time-out?

If your child argues about or objects to time-out, calmly state an additional consequence if he does not immediately comply. You might say, for instance, that he will see no TV for the rest of the day or that he will have to go to bed a half hour early. And if he chooses to refuse the time-out, make sure to follow through with your additional consequence. Although it is permissible to lead your child firmly by the hand or shoulder to the time-out spot, it is not advisable to chase after him or physically drag him there. Nor is it a good idea to argue with your child about whether or not he should go to time-out.

What should I be doing while my child is in time-out?

While your child is in time-out, you should be ignoring him as much as possible. If he yells, screams, or throws a temper tantrum while in time-out, let your timer do the talking. Be consistent in not starting the timer until your child is sitting quietly. And if he starts to talk, whine, yell, or scream after your timing has started, calmly and silently reset the timer for another 5 minutes. Under no circumstances should you or any other family member talk to your child while he is in time-out, nor should you or anyone else be nearby watching him. While in time-out, your child should be *ignored*.

What should I do if my child makes a mess while in time-out?

Some children may get upset about being in time-out and may respond by making a mess. If this happens with your child, administer a logical consequence. For example, if he has drawn on or dirtied the walls, let him know that, following time-out, he will have to clean up the mess. If the child breaks or destroys the time-out chair, let him know that he will have to help replace it out of his allowance money. You can avoid some complications by keeping drawing materials away from a child in time-out and by using a sturdy chair or the bottom of a staircase as the time-out spot.

What should I do after the timer signals an end to the time-out?

When the timer signals the end of the 5-minute time-out, calmly tell your child that he may leave the time-out spot. Never apologize to your child for putting him into time-out—after all, it was the child's choice to misbehave. Also, do not require your child to apologize or express regret in order to be able to leave the time-out spot. If, however, the child happens to apologize spontaneously, be sure to give positive attention to his apology—for example, saying, "Thank you for telling me you are sorry for what you did."

If your child went into time-out because of disobedient behavior (such as refusing to pick up his toys or turn off the

TV), it is very important to repeat your original command the moment time-out ends. If he again refuses to obey, immediately send him back to time-out. If, on the other hand, he obeys your command, give him some verbal praise, such as "I like it when you do what I ask." At first this sequence may need to be repeated several times; the child may continue to disobey even after a time-out. But if you are consistent and do not give up, eventually your child will learn that you mean business and that he needs to comply in order to avoid future time-outs.

If your child went to time-out for some reason other than disobeying a command, then you should look for the very next opportunity to catch his good behavior. This will assure him that you are not holding a grudge and that you still want to give him positive attention for appropriate behavior.

What should I do if my child misbehaves outside of the home?

If your child misbehaves when you are away from home—for instance, at the grocery store or at a neighbor's—calmly point out the misbehavior and add that, if the misbehavior continues, she will have a time-out immediately after you get home. If she continues to misbehave, be sure to follow through with the time-out when you do get home. Some parents find it helpful to make "time-out tickets," strips of paper with the words "One 5-Minute Time-Out" written on them, for use outside the home. When the child misbehaves away from home, she is given one of these time-out tickets, which must be paid for with a 5-minute time-out immediately upon arrival at home. (Two tickets would result in 10 minutes of time-out.)

Another way to manage misbehavior outside the home is to give a time-out on the spot. You warn the child that she must immediately cease the misbehavior or she will receive a time-out. If she does not comply with the warning, you then find a secluded spot where she must stay for 5 minutes. A corner in your neighbor's house, the back seat of your car, or a corner of the store can be used for this purpose. When in a park or some other outdoor setting, you may want to try what one of the authors does—that is, designate a particular tree as a time-out tree where his children must stand if they misbehave.

I know what's going to happen with my child. He's going to say, "Fine! Put me in time-out! I don't care!" What should I do when he says this?

Some children may try to manipulate their parents by saying that time-out doesn't faze them and that it will never make them behave. Such children may even taunt their parents by saying, "Go ahead! Put me in time-out! I like going to time-out!" Try not to be upset by such statements. Instead, attempt to stay calm and follow through with the time-out. Don't give in to this kind of manipulation.

Your child may also attempt to avoid time-out by promising to obey your request after you have issued the time-out. If this occurs, it is very important that he still go directly to time-out. He will have another opportunity to obey your request after the time-out is completed.

Will time-out cause an immediate improvement in my child's behavior?

If you decide to try time-out, do not expect immediate improvement in your child's behavior. In fact, in the short run, you may even observe an increase in misbehavior. Your child may express her anger at your use of time-out by saying that she dislikes or even hates you. Such behavior will probably mean that your child is testing your limits to see if you are sincere. Thus, as with other child management techniques, it is extremely important to use time-out consistently and to follow through once you begin to use it. If the technique is used correctly and consistently, misbehavior usually begins to decrease in about 1 to 2 weeks.

Once I start using time-out, must I keep on using the other techniques you talked about in earlier chapters?

Yes! It is *absolutely essential* that every behavior change program include ways to provide positive reinforcement for the appropriate behavior that you would like to see replace the misbehavior. We have already talked about ways to do this—including catching your child's good behavior and using star charts. The important thing is never to use time-out by itself. It should always be coupled with techniques that focus on increasing appropriate behavior.

CHAPTER EIGHT

Compliance Training: How to Get Your Child to Do What You Ask

Perhaps the most common complaint heard from parents of children with ADHD is that their children do not do what they are asked to do. There are several reasons for this. First, children with ADHD have more difficulty than other children attending to instructions. Second, when these children do attend to instructions, they frequently get distracted before they can complete the task they were asked to do. And third, many children with ADHD have learned that noncompliance pays off—that is, their parents frequently find it easier to do something themselves than to try to get the child to do it. This chapter will offer you a program for dealing with disobedience in a child with ADHD. If your child is not among those who are frequently disobedient, then thank your lucky stars and skip the rest of the chapter. But for most parents, this chapter may be among the most important in the book.

What do you mean by compliance training?

It is not only reasonable for you to expect that your children do what you tell them to do, it is your responsibility as a parent to ensure that this happens. Children who have learned to obey their parents generally tend also to obey other important adults in their lives, such as teachers, police officers, and babysitters. Such children also generally follow rules. And research has clearly shown that children who have learned to follow rules are happier, friendlier, and more energetic than children who have not. The way to teach children to follow rules is to teach them to do what you tell them *the very first time.* This is what compliance training is all about.

How do I go about compliance training?

The first step is to recognize two basic biological differences between your child with ADHD and other children. First, children with ADHD generally have difficulty paying attention to a long sequence of instructions or commands. And second, children with ADHD have difficulty sustaining their effort for long periods—especially when attempting to complete tasks that are imposed upon them by others. Because of these two biological difficulties, children with ADHD are often noncompliant not because they want to be disobedient, but because their ADHD gets in the way of their obedience. Consequently, if parents change the way they give commands to a child with ADHD, they are likely to see some increase in obedient behavior.

How exactly should I give commands to my child with ADHD?

The first principle is to give commands to your child *one at a time.* Parents generally use what are called "chain commands" in giving instructions to their children. A chain command happens when a number of single commands are grouped into one long command. For example, it would not be uncommon to hear a parent say, "Johnny, turn off the TV and then go upstairs and change your shirt to the blue one I left on your bed, and then go wash your hands and come down for dinner." Although a child without ADHD might be able to keep track of such a series of commands, children with ADHD find it very difficult both to pay attention to and to remember commands in long strings. Consequently, they frequently miss some parts of the chain command or place them out of order. For a child with ADHD, you need to break these long chain commands into smaller parts. Using the example just mentioned, you might say, "Johnny, it's time for dinner. Now, first I want you to turn off the TV." Once Johnny has turned off the TV, you can then say, "Good! You turned off the TV just like I asked! Now go upstairs and change into the blue shirt I left on your bed." After Johnny completes this task, you can say, "Good! You changed your shirt just like I asked you to do! Now I want you to go and wash your hands"—and so forth. The idea is simply to give one command at a time.

A second important principle in giving commands is to *be specific*. Avoid vague commands like "Johnny! Let's get going!" Rather, you need to specify very precisely what it is you want Johnny to do: "Johnny! It's time to get ready for bed. First, I want you to go change into your pajamas." (Remember: One command at a time!)

A third important principle in giving commands is to *give mostly "go" commands*, not "stop" commands. That is, avoid saying things like "Johnny! Stop jumping on the couch!" Instead, give commands that tell Johnny what he *should* be doing. In this example you might say, "Johnny, please sit on the couch when you are watching TV." The reason for this principle is that if you give a stop command, Johnny can comply with it by doing something equally inappropriate— for example, he could stop jumping on the couch by jumping instead on the easy chair! But with a go command, he can be compliant only by doing exactly as you say.

A fourth important principle in giving commands is to *tell your child to do something*, rather than asking him to do it. Many parents make the mistake of phrasing a command as a question or, worse yet, as a request for a favor. They say things like "Johnny, could you do me a favor and go upstairs and clean your room?" It is certainly fine to ask your child to do you a favor if you really mean it as a favor. But if you really intend for him to go upstairs and clean his room *now*, you should state it as a command: "Johnny, I want you to go upstairs and clean your room now." If the command is a question rather than a statement, your child can always say no.

How can I know whether I'm giving the right sort of commands?

One way to develop the habit of giving mostly good commands to your child is to chart the quality of your commands. You can do this easily with a small index card or slip of paper divided in half vertically with a line down the middle. At the top of this record write "Good command" on the left and "Poor command" on the right. (See the example in Figure 6.)

Figure 6   Sample Good Commands/Poor Commands Record

Date ___ *October 10* ___   Time ___ *3-4 P.M.* ___

Good command	Poor command
IIII	I

Then choose an hour each day when you are most likely to be around your child and judge the quality of each command that you give him, tallying it on the appropriate side of the record. That is, if your command was a single command (not part of a chain), was specific about what you wanted your child to do, was a "go" command, and was phrased as a command and not a question, then you can tally it on the record as a good command. But if you gave more than one command at a time, were vague about what you wanted your child to do, told your child to stop doing something rather than what to start doing, or stated your command as a question, then you should record the command as a poor one. Continue charting your command behavior until at least 70 percent of your commands are in the good command category for at least 3 days in a row. The way in which you obtain this percentage per day is to divide the number of tally marks in the good commands column by the total number of tally marks on your record for that day (that is, the total number of commands you recorded in both the good and poor command columns).

What do I do after I reach 3 days in a row of at least 70 percent of my commands being in the good command category?

Once you have reached the 70 percent level for good parent commands, the next step is to begin charting how often your child obeys and disobeys your commands. As you did in charting your commands, choose a certain hour of the day and prepare an index card or slip of paper (see Figure 7 for an example). For that hour, record how often your child complies with your commands the very first time and how often he does not comply. For the purpose of charting, compliance is defined as beginning to do what you ask within 5 seconds of your command. And try to remember to give good quality commands.

What if my child continues to disobey?

If you are lucky, you may find that once you have begun giving mostly good quality commands, your child will be complying with most of them. If this is so, then you can

Figure 7   Sample Compliance With Commands Record

Date _____ *October 10* _____   Time _____ *3-4 P.M.* _____

Complied with command	Disobeyed command
III	*II*

skip the rest of this chapter. However, this is usually not the case. Rather, most parents find that, even though they are generally giving good quality commands, their child continues to disobey frequently. If this is the case with your child, you will need to add two more things to your compliance training program.

First, you should set up a special star chart for times when your child complies immediately without a fuss. That is, you should catch your child obeying your commands. (You might want to review chapter 5 for ideas on how to do this.) Second, you need to use time-out as a mild discipline for occasions when your child does not comply.

How do I tell my child about this program?

First, explain that you will be awarding stars for times when your child does what you ask *the very first time without a fuss.* Also set up a system for exchanging the stars for rewards— such as small amounts of money, extra stay-up time at night, a special family activity, or some other small treat that is not too extravagant. (Sometimes it is helpful to make a list of possible rewards that your child can work to earn, specifying how many stars each item is worth.) Inform your child that if he doesn't do what you ask the very first time, you will repeat your command but with a warning that, if he doesn't comply immediately, the result will be a time-out. If your child complies only following the warning, do not give him a star—compliance at this point only allows him to avoid a time-out. And if he disregards the warning, then you should send him to time-out. Of course, as we stressed in chapter 7 on time-out, you should repeat your command after the time-out is completed so that your child has another chance to comply (or to learn that further noncompliance only results in another time-out). Do not add a star to your child's chart for obeying your command following a time-out. His only opportunity to be rewarded is to comply *the very first time.*

Another one of my problems is getting my child to follow rules when I'm not around. What do I do about that?

Most families have a set of general household rules that every family member is expected to follow. Unfortunately, these rules are typically not defined very clearly, and they are often enforced inconsistently. The first step in getting your child to obey general household rules is to write them down. This will help you more clearly define what behaviors you will expect of every family member—including your child with ADHD. A good way to start this process is to call a family meeting and have everyone suggest one rule that should be included on the list. The parents, of course, are to be the final judges, but it will be very helpful if you take every suggestion seriously.

After collecting suggestions and listing the rules, post them in a highly visible place—for instance, on the refrigerator door or on a kitchen cabinet. If you notice that your child with ADHD is having particular difficulty with one or more of the rules, you can set up a specific behavior change program for increasing compliance with that rule. For example, you might decide that your child can earn extra stay-up time for every day that she does not leave dirty dishes in the family room but that she must go to bed a half hour early every day you find one of her dirty dishes left behind. Once everyone is complying with this set of household rules, you can call another family meeting to discuss adding more rules to the list.

Does compliance training really work?

You bet! But it takes time—and it works only when there is a generally positive family atmosphere. That is, it may be tempting only to discipline for instances of disobedience and to ignore (whether intentionally or unintentionally) instances of compliant behavior. But if you first change the way you give commands to your child and then add rewards for compliance and mild negative consequences for noncompliance, it is likely that your child will become much more obedient and cooperative around the home.

CHAPTER NINE

Helping the Teenager Who Has Attention Deficit Hyperactivity Disorder

You may be wondering what your child with ADHD will be like when she becomes a teenager. For many years, it was thought that children with ADHD gradually outgrew the disorder as they reached the teenage years. We now know, however, that for many individuals this is not the case. Although the severity of ADHD symptoms often does decrease as children approach the teens, many continue to have significant problems with both paying attention and delaying impulses. Some children with ADHD also continue to have difficulty achieving well in school, and many continue to have trouble getting along with authority figures like parents, teachers, and employers. Consequently, continued help may be necessary for many persons with ADHD throughout the teen years.

What should I do if my child with ADHD continues to have behavior problems when she becomes a teenager?

Many of the parenting techniques discussed thus far can be slightly modified for use with the teenager who has ADHD. For example, as with a younger child, whenever your teenager is engaging in some inappropriate behavior, you should first observe and chart that behavior to find out how often it is occurring and whether or not it needs changing. However, you may not want to display a teenager's recording chart in a conspicuous place, as this may be embarrassing for her. Similarly, although the principles of positive reinforcement for appropriate behavior and consistent limit setting for inappropriate behavior will continue to be important, star charts and time-out are not appropriate techniques to use with a teenager.

As your child with ADHD grows into her teenage years, she will begin to show an increased desire for independence. As this happens, it will be important to allow her to earn additional responsibilities that will help prepare her for some of the responsibilities of adulthood. Let your teenager practice some of the skills necessary for handling the responsibilities of adult life.

Should my teenager with ADHD receive psychostimulant medication?

Some teenagers with ADHD benefit from psychostimulant medication, and others do not. As with a younger child, a well-monitored trial of psychostimulant medication will be necessary to determine whether it is right for your teenager. Of course, you should consult the young person's physician regarding the appropriateness of psychostimulant medication. If such medication is prescribed, its use should be continually and closely monitored by the physician.

Are there any special behavior management techniques that I can use with my teenager who has ADHD?

One very useful technique that is appropriate for teenagers with ADHD is called a *behavior contract*. This is an agreement between the parents and the young person concerning behavior to be changed and consequences to be delivered for specific appropriate and inappropriate behaviors. The terms of this contract are actively negotiated and agreed upon by both the parents and their teenager; they are then written down and signed by everyone involved. Specific positive reinforcers are determined for specified appropriate behaviors, and specific negative consequences are determined for specified inappropriate behaviors. Figure 8 shows a sample behavior contract.

If I decide to use a behavior contract with my teenager, can't I just decide on the terms of the contract myself?

Absolutely not! It is very important that you involve your teenager in the negotiation process. If a young person is made to feel that he has important ideas and opinions about what behaviors need to be changed, how to change them, and what kinds of consequences should be specified in the

Figure 8   Sample Behavior Contract

I, _____Sarah Jones_____, agree to perform the

following behavior:

I will be home by 6:00 P.M. Sunday through Thursday, and by

10:00 P.M. Friday and Saturday.

_____

_____

_____

If I am successful in performing this behavior, then I will receive:

Daily Reward: 30 minutes of extra telephone time for each day

I am home on time.

Weekly Reward: 1 hour of extra time beyond curfew on a Friday

or Saturday evening (or) privilege of having a friend sleep

over on a Friday or Saturday evening.

If I am unsuccessful in performing this behavior, then I will not receive:

Telephone time for that day.

_____

_____

_____

_____

I agree to follow the terms of this contract the best I can.

Signature _Sarah Jones_ (Teenager)   Date _August 6, 1991_

Signature _Pamela Jones_ (Parent)   Date _August 6, 1991_ contract, then he will be more likely to obey the terms of the contract. Also, by involving your teenager in the negotiation process, you help him learn effective problem-solving methods. He may develop a better understanding of ways to generate alternative solutions to problems and the likely consequences of those solutions.

How do I go about setting up a behavior contract with my teenager?

First, sit down with your teenager and calmly describe, as clearly and specifically as you can, the behavior that is troubling you. Explain that you think things would be more pleasant at home if the particular behavior changed. Then ask your teenager to share his ideas about this behavior. He may simply not know that you are concerned about it. If this is the case, then making him aware of your concerns may be enough to change the behavior. However, if this does not adequately address the problem, you will need to proceed with a behavior contract.

What should I do after I have obtained my teenager's opinion about the problem behavior?

Explain that you have a plan, called a behavior contract, that may help him change the inappropriate behavior so that life will go more smoothly at home. As precisely as possible, describe the appropriate behavior that you would like your teenager to substitute for the inappropriate one. You might say, "Instead of playing your stereo so loudly when I'm trying to concentrate on my office work, I would like you to keep the volume low with your door shut after 7:00 in the evening"; or you might say, "Instead of leaving your school books and schoolwork on the kitchen counter when I am trying to get dinner ready, I would appreciate your taking all of your things to your room when you get home from school." Then ask your teenager if he is able to perform the behavior that you are requesting; there may be times when he is unable, for good reasons, to do as you ask. Listen carefully to such reasons and then determine whether they are indeed valid.

Make it clear to your teenager that a behavior contract means working together to determine a plan for changing his behavior. Part of the plan is a written contract specifying the rewards and consequences for appropriate and inappropriate behaviors. At this point, you should start to negotiate the conditions of the contract, including incentives to be earned on a daily and weekly basis.

What are some examples of daily and weekly incentives?

Daily incentives should consist of small rewards, and weekly incentives should consist of more significant ones. For instance, if your teenager performs the desired behavior on a certain day, the daily reward may be use of the family car for that evening or a small, predetermined amount of money. The larger rewards should be reserved for the attainment of weekly goals, such as engaging in the desired behavior a certain number of times during that week. A weekly reward might be permission to sleep over at a friend's house or attend a party.

Negative consequences, however, should be given only on a daily, not on a weekly, basis. In addition, they should be somewhat mild, such as limited television time for that day or loss of phone privileges that evening. The reason for using only mild, daily negative consequences is so that the young person's participation in the contract will be motivated primarily by enthusiasm to earn positive rewards, rather than by a desire to avoid negative consequences.

Is charting important even for this kind of program?

Yes. It is quite important to chart your teenager's behavior when using a behavior contract. As with any behavior change program, charting at the outset will help you decide how to try to change the inappropriate behavior, and charting while the behavior contract is in progress will help you determine whether or not the behavior is improving. For example, suppose you want your teenager to improve in setting the dinner table without being reminded. First, chart this behavior to find out how often it is already occurring. You can then use this information to begin to require small increases in the behavior. You might discover that your teenager only sets the dinner table once a week without a reminder, so you might establish a weekly goal that he set the table twice a week to earn his reward for that week. If this weekly goal is met, it can be increased for the next week to setting the table three times without a reminder, and so on. Remember, you want to increase the behavioral demands of the contract slowly: Don't demand perfect behavior during the first week.

Should I make all the rules required for contract changes?

No. When you want to increase the demands of the contract, sit down with your teenager to renegotiate the terms. He should have just as much input into contract changes as he did when the original contract was devised. You can explain to your teenager that he has been doing so well that he deserves some extra responsibilities, and he will now be rewarded if he is able to handle these added responsibilities. Increases in behavioral demands should occur at a point when your teenager is easily fulfilling the terms of the contract.

Is it important to provide immediate feedback to my teenager when he engages in the behaviors specified in the contract?

Yes. When your teenager performs the appropriate behaviors outlined in the contract, it is *vital* that you provide the rewards that the contract specifies and that you also provide positive attention and praise at the same time. When your teenager exhibits the inappropriate behaviors named in the contract, state the consequences in a calm and matter-of-fact manner, with little lecturing or scolding. In either case, feedback should be given as quickly as possible after the behavior has occurred.

Is behavior contracting helpful for all teenagers with ADHD?

Often, the problems of teenagers are so complex and difficult to manage that a behavior contract may not be sufficient to change inappropriate behavior. Resources listed in the bibliography and reference list at the end of this book describe additional techniques for promoting behavior change. If your teenager's problems are particularly severe (for instance, if drug or alcohol abuse is involved, or if your teenager has a history of running away from home), then you will probably need the help of a psychologist or other mental health professional.

CHAPTER TEN

Daily Home Report Cards: A Home-Based Program for Improving School Behavior

The principles that we have outlined for improving behavior in the home can also help your child to behave better at school. However, school-related behavior problems, compared to misbehavior in the home, are a bit more difficult to deal with for several reasons. First, teachers have fewer potential reinforcers to call on because the most powerful incentives and motivators for children, such as extra stay-up time at night or family activities, are available only in the home. Second, given that 20 to 30 students may be in each classroom, teachers are less able than parents to spend a great deal of time with one child. And third, teachers are often reluctant to reward just one student for fear that others will feel resentful and react negatively toward the child. Despite these added difficulties, there are some procedures that can help improve the school behavior of a child with ADHD. One relatively simple home-based program for improving your child's behavior at school is called a *daily home report card*.

What is a daily home report card?

Report cards have traditionally been used as a way of providing feedback to parents about their child's school behavior and achievement. For children with ADHD, however, the traditional report card system is inadequate because the feedback is usually infrequent (report cards are typically issued just three or four times per year). In

addition, when more frequent feedback is provided, perhaps through notes or phone calls from the teacher, it tends
to focus on a child's misbehavior or poor performance.
Rarely do teachers have the time to write extensive notes or
call parents to tell them about their child's appropriate
behavior.

In contrast, daily home report cards are sent home to the
parents *each and every school day.* They include ratings of
both the positive and negative aspects of the child's behavior for that day. The parents then provide consequences at
home for school behavior that has occurred on that day—
giving the child positive reinforcement for good ratings and
negative consequences for poor ratings. Thus, both the child
and the parents are able to receive daily feedback about
school behavior, rather than waiting until months after the
behavior may have occurred.

What kinds of behaviors can be improved by use of a daily home report card system?

Daily home report cards can improve behaviors that are
important for success in school, such as following teachers'
instructions, obeying requests, completing schoolwork, raising a hand before talking in class, and getting along with
other children. Strengthening such behaviors may help
some children with ADHD be more open to what is being
taught and may thus increase their success in schoolwork.
In other words, if a child is behaving well and attending to
her work, she will likely have more opportunity to learn
what is being taught; however, if she is misbehaving and
not attending to her work, she will be spending little time
learning new material.

What kinds of behaviors cannot be improved through daily home report cards?

Although a daily home report card system can be very
helpful in improving the school behavior of a child with
ADHD, it does have limits. Most important, daily home
report cards are not designed to "cure" specific learning
disabilities in such areas as spelling, reading, or arithmetic.
These problems typically need to be managed by a special
education professional who has been trained in particular
resource methods. In addition, the daily home report card

system is not intended for use with severely emotionally disturbed children; these children are likely to need more intensive school-based programs. Finally, daily home report cards are not meant to replace medication in increasing the child's ability to pay attention. Although some children with ADHD may show improved ability to pay attention with the use of daily home report cards, many will still require medication to increase the ability to concentrate in class for long periods. (Our own research, however, has indicated that the daily home report card system may allow a child to manage on a lower dose of medication.)

How do I go about setting up a daily home report card system?

First, talk with your child's teacher about your desire to develop and implement such a system. Then, both you and the teacher should develop a reasonable system for transmitting daily behavior reports for your child. It is better and easier to develop this system by sitting down together than by talking on the telephone.

Because teachers deal with many students every day, the daily home report card should be as brief as possible. If the teacher must spend more than a minute or two each day filling it out, you are unlikely to receive consistent feedback. Much of the time, a simple daily rating of 1 to 5 for overall behavior, where 1 = very poor, 2 = poor, 3 = fair, 4 = good, and 5 = excellent, will be adequate. Sometimes, however, it will be necessary to be more specific about the behaviors that you want to improve, such as completing classroom assignments, not disturbing other students while they work, participating during class discussions, staying seated during class, raising a hand before talking, and getting along with other children. When more specific behaviors are being worked on, each behavior would receive a separate 1-to-5 rating on the daily card. If you decide to work on specific behaviors, we suggest that you focus on only one or two behaviors at a time. Sometimes it might also be useful to have the teacher rate your child once in the morning and once in the afternoon.

Where does my child's teacher make these ratings?

The daily ratings can be made on index cards or slips of paper that your child brings home every day. It is best to supply the teacher with a stack of prepared cards or slips on which to record the ratings. For an overall behavior rating, you need only write your child's name on the top and indicate places for the teacher to write the date of the rating and the daily rating itself. If you are working on specific behaviors, you should list the behaviors and indicate a place to rate each one. And if the teacher is rating your child twice a day, the report card can be divided in half. (Examples of daily home report cards are shown in Figure 9.) Ask your child's teacher to write any additional comments on the back of the card and to sign at the bottom to reduce the possibility that your child will write down the rating himself. If your child attends more than one classroom during the school day, you may either ask each teacher to complete a separate card or divide the card into separate class periods, with each teacher providing a rating for the time spent with your child.

Do I tell my child about this daily home report card system?

Yes, your child should be fully informed about this system. Explain the rating scale and stress that the teacher will be sending the report card to you each and every day. Be sure to describe specifically what kinds of appropriate behaviors will lead to good ratings and what kinds of inappropriate behaviors will lead to poor ratings, as some children may not understand the distinction clearly. The teacher may also want to talk with your child about how he can earn good and poor ratings. It is vital that parents, teachers, and child have a mutual and very clear understanding about the kinds of behaviors that will result in good and poor ratings. Let your child know the rewards he can earn by bringing home good ratings as well as the negative consequences that will be applied when he brings home poor ones.

So, the ratings from the daily home report card will be used to determine consequences for my child?

Exactly right! In deciding what rewards to offer for good ratings, you might first ask your child what kinds of reinforcers he would like to earn. It is good to develop a list of both daily and weekly rewards. The daily rewards, used for rewarding acceptable daily ratings, should be relatively small (for example, quarters, pencils, pens, small pads of

Figure 9   Sample Daily Home Report Cards

Sample A (for overall behavior)

Child's name ___*Gene*___   Date ___*December 2*___

Daily rating (circle)

very poor   excellent

(1)   2   3   4   5

Teacher's signature ___*D. M. Danielson*___

Sample B (for overall behavior)

Child's name ___*Jill*___   Date ___*December 2*___

Morning rating (circle)   **Afternoon rating (circle)**

very poor   excellent   very poor   excellent

1   2   (3)   4   5   1   2   3   (4)   5

Teacher's signature ___*D. M. Danielson*___

Sample C (for specific behaviors)

Child's name ___*Jeff*___   Date ___*December 2*___

Behavior	**Rating**

| | very poor   excellent |

1. ___*Completing assignments*___   1   2   (3)   4   5

2. ___*Staying seated*___   1   (2)   3   4   5

Teacher's signature ___*D. M. Danielson*___

paper, or extra stay-up time at night). The weekly rewards, given when the child has achieved an acceptable number of daily ratings for the week, can be larger (for example, a picnic in the park or a videotape rental of the child's choice). As with all positive reinforcement, when your child earns rewards for good ratings, always be sure to give social reinforcement, such as verbal praise, as well.

Negative consequences for poor ratings (ratings of 1 or 2) should not be severe, as it is more effective for your child to try his best as a way to earn rewards. For example, do not respond to a single day's bad ratings by putting your child on restriction for a week or a month (four acceptable daily report cards in any single week are actually quite commendable). Instead, use smaller negative consequences like an earlier bedtime or loss of dessert after dinner for that night. Moreover, negative consequences should be applied only for a poor daily rating and never for falling short of a weekly goal. And remember, the most important and effective tactic of any behavior change program, including daily home report cards, is to reward appropriate behavior.

How do I determine which ratings will earn rewards for my child?

As we discussed in earlier chapters, you should work from a baseline. That is, you should first collect daily home report card ratings for a week to find out what kind of behavior your child is currently displaying in school. Then proceed with small steps toward achievement of better behavioral ratings. For instance, when using the 1-to-5 rating system in which 1 = very poor and 5 = excellent, obtain an average rating for the week by adding all daily ratings and dividing the sum by the number of daily ratings that were sent home. Then, if your child's average weekly rating is 1.5, for example, you can require a rating of 2 for a daily reward. You can slowly begin to increase the rating that is required for your child to earn the reward. Be careful, however, not to require too great an improvement over the baseline ratings, for if you do your child may become frustrated and discouraged with the program. For instance, in the example just mentioned, it would be a mistake to begin immediately requiring ratings of 4. In addition, because nobody is perfect, you should never require that your child obtain daily ratings of 5 in order to be rewarded.

If the daily report card includes ratings on several behaviors, how do I determine when to reward my child?

In this case, simply use the average rating for each day during the baseline period to find out what rating should be rewarded. For example, suppose the behaviors being rated are staying seated and getting along with other children. Further suppose that, on the first day, your child was rated 2 for staying seated and 4 for getting along with other children. The average rating for that day would be 3 (add the ratings of 2 and 4, then divide the sum by the number of ratings made—in this case 2). Obtain an average rating for each day of that week, and then divide the sum of these numbers by 5 (the number of school days in the week) for the average daily rating. Suppose, for example, that average is 2.4; you can begin by offering a daily reward if, and only if, your child comes home with a daily average rating of at least 3.

What should I do if my child loses the daily home report card or forgets to bring it home?

If your child loses the daily home report card, forgets to bring it home, chooses not to bring it home, or forges a rating, then you should treat this as if he had brought home a rating of 1 (that is, the worst possible rating). If the child says that his teacher did not give him a report card to bring home, let him know that it is his responsibility to obtain the report card from the teacher and that he may have to remind the teacher at the end of the day, as teachers are often quite preoccupied at that time.

How long must I keep using this daily home report card system?

As your child reaches a satisfactory level of behavioral ratings, the card can be sent home less frequently as a way of slowly phasing out the daily report card system. For instance, the card could be sent home every other day for a 2- to 3-week period, then once a week for 1 to 2 weeks, then once every other week, and finally not at all. If you are in the process of discontinuing, or have discontinued, the home report card and your child's misbehavior increases, simply start using the system again on a daily basis.

Is it all right occasionally to give my child the reward if he just barely misses his daily rating goal?

> No. No. No. If you give your child a daily or weekly reward when he falls short of his goal, then you will be teaching him that he can obtain rewards without really earning them. In fact, if you give in and provide an unearned reward, your child might even begin to decrease his effort to improve his behavior because he will have discovered that he doesn't need to work as hard to obtain the positive reinforcer.

Must I give a reward every time my child meets his rating goal and discipline him every time he doesn't meet his goal?

> Yes. Yes. Yes. It is crucial that both you and your child's teacher be consistent with this program. If you are inconsistent, it is quite likely that the child's inappropriate school behavior will continue or even become worse. And don't be too easily discouraged if the home report card system does not result in immediate improvements in behavior. Remember, this kind of program will take some time to work because the consequences for school behavior cannot be administered as quickly as for home behavior.

CHAPTER ELEVEN

Summary and Troubleshooting

In this book, we have introduced a number of techniques for increasing the appropriate behavior and decreasing the inappropriate behavior of your child with ADHD. We are confident that, with these techniques, you now have the basic tools for helping your child become more successful both at home and in the classroom. Still, most parents find it quite challenging to combine these techniques to address a specific behavior problem with their child. Indeed, planning effective behavior management programs is a skill that requires much practice. In this chapter, we will present a plan for using the various techniques when future behavior problems arise.

How do I go about putting together all of these different behavior management techniques for a specific behavior problem my child may be having?

Following is a summary of the steps you should take when you are faced with a particular behavior problem and want to develop a behavior change program for your child.

STEP 1 _____

Decide exactly what your child is doing that troubles you. *Be specific.* That is, try to describe the behavior in such a way that you will be able to count the instances of it. For example, do not say, "My child is irresponsible"; rather, say, "My child frequently forgets to hand in her homework at school."

STEP 2 _____

Determine what you want your child to do *instead of* the inappropriate behavior. In other words, decide what appropriate

behavior you would like your child to substitute for the behavior that is now troubling you. For example, if your child
frequently forgets to hand in her homework at school, the
alternative appropriate behavior is to hand in her homework
regularly.

STEP 3 _____

Make a chart and record every time your child displays the
inappropriate behavior *and* every time she displays the
appropriate behavior that you want her to develop instead.
Continue this charting for at least 1 week. As we pointed
out in chapter 5, on increasing appropriate behavior, this
information is called a baseline. It will tell you how often
your child is currently engaging in both the inappropriate
and the appropriate behavior so that you can decide
whether or not the behavior needs to be changed.

STEP 4 _____

After collecting this baseline information, talk with your child
about the problem behavior. Describe the specific behavior
you think is inappropriate; then tell your child what you
would like her to do instead. Be *very specific* about the appropriate behavior you would like your child to substitute for
the inappropriate one. It is also helpful at this point to ask
for your child's ideas on how you might assist her in changing her behavior. This can help your child to feel that she is
a part of the decision, and she may be more willing to work
with you (rather than against you) in the process of
behavior change.

STEP 5 _____

Begin using a star chart to reward your child for the appropriate behavior that you want to substitute for the inappropriate behavior. Many parents find it useful to keep a star
chart in the home regularly so that when a behavior problem arises, they can just add the appropriate "replacement"
behavior to the list of things that the child can do to earn a
star. As we emphasized in the discussion on catching your
child's good behavior (chapter 5), whenever you do award a
star, be sure also to give verbal messages that emphasize
your child's accomplishment.

Initially, you may sometimes need to use a material reward, a special activity reward, or an extra privilege to supplement the star chart. Depending upon the behavior you are working on, you may want to establish both daily and weekly rewards as incentives for more appropriate behavior. The daily rewards should be small, whereas weekly rewards can be more significant.

Remember, as you work through a behavior change program, that you should always proceed in small steps: That is, as you raise your child's daily and/or weekly goals, you should require behavioral improvements a little at a time. Beware of requiring improvements that are too great. Indeed, asking the child to improve too quickly is one of the most common mistakes parents make. In addition, at the beginning of any behavior change program, it will be necessary to reinforce the appropriate behavior as consistently and immediately as possible. Then, as your child's behavior improves, you can gradually start to deemphasize the material, activity, or extra privilege rewards and replace them with social praise and attention.

STEP 6

If the use of a star chart does not significantly improve a misbehavior, then also begin to ignore the inappropriate behavior to see if it will reduce in frequency, intensity, or duration. Ignoring will be especially effective either if the misbehavior is an attention-getting strategy or if there is a natural consequence that will reduce the misbehavior. Ignoring is generally *not* effective, however, if the misbehavior allows your child to avoid doing something that she was told to do. Thus, ignoring instances of noncompliance is generally not very effective—in fact, ignoring noncompliance will probably make things even worse.

STEP 7

If the inappropriate behavior continues despite repeated and consistent attempts to ignore it, try giving a logical consequence for the inappropriate behavior, such as response cost, overcorrection, or positive practice. (Refer to chapter 6 for examples of these different types of logical consequences.)

STEP 8 _____

If logical consequences do not significantly decrease the in-appropriate behavior, or if you cannot think of a meaningful logical consequence for a particular misbehavior, then try using time-out if your child is between the ages of 3 and 10 (see chapter 7). For an older child, you will want to rely more and more upon behavior contracts for managing behavior. (Refer to chapter 9 for guidance on using behavior contracts with older children.)

How will I know if a particular behavior change program is working?

You will be able to tell whether a behavior change program is working by looking at your child's behavior charts and comparing your baseline information with the information that you obtain as you introduce the different behavior management techniques. For example, if the baseline chart shows that your child was originally obeying 40 percent of your commands, look to see whether he is now obeying more or less often. If the percentage has risen to, say, 80 percent, then you know that your behavior change program is working. If the percentage has remained about the same or has decreased, then it is time to go back to the drawing board.

Must I really keep charting my child's behavior throughout the behavior change program? Won't I just be able to tell whether or not her behavior is getting better without a chart?

It will be very tempting either to start a behavior change project without first charting a baseline or to give up on charting once the behavior change program is in place. Do not give in to either of these temptations. Rather, you should continue to chart your child's behavior throughout the process. This way, you can look at your charts as the weeks pass to determine objectively whether things are im-proving, rather than relying on momentary impressions or guesswork. And the problem with guessing is that you might be wrong—which might lead you either to give up on a program that is, in fact, working or to continue with a program that is not helping or is making things even worse.

What if I look at my weekly charts and find that things really aren't getting any better?

If the weekly behavior charts indicate that your child's behavior is not improving, then you need to ask yourself the following questions:

1. Am I spending 10 or 15 minutes of Very Special Time with my child every day?

Remember, Very Special Time should continue even if you are not currently working on a specific behavior change program.

2. Am I paying attention to the appropriate behavior that I want my child to develop instead of the inappropriate behavior?

Always praise your child for engaging in the appropriate behavior as well as marking it down on a behavior chart.

3. For appropriate behavior, am I using rewards that are important to my child?

Be sure that the reinforcers you are using are not too weak; in other words, the rewards you give should be of importance and interest to your child. The best way to determine what these rewards might be is to ask your child at the beginning of the behavior change program what he would like to earn for changing the behavior.

4. Am I nagging, lecturing, or criticizing my child for inappropriate behavior?

Remember, any attention you give to your child's misbehavior may inadvertently be reinforcing it. Either ignore misbehavior or use small, timely negative consequences (such as time-out) delivered in a matter-of-fact manner.

5. Am I consistently disciplining my child when he does misbehave?

If you don't discipline your child every single time he misbehaves, he will tend to focus on the times you don't discipline him rather than on the times you do. That is, he will learn that often he can get away with misbehavior. *Never give your child a warning about some discipline (such as a* time-out or a logical consequence) and then "forget" to follow through. This only teaches your child that you do not mean what you say. *Discipline must be consistent to be effective!*

6. Am I waiting too long before I discipline my child?

Negative consequences are most effective when they immediately follow a misbehavior. The longer you wait, the less effective the discipline will be.

7. When I give a command or instruction to my child, am I giving only one instruction at a time? Am I waiting until my child finishes obeying that instruction before I give another command or instruction?

A child with ADHD will have a difficult time attending to and remembering more than one command at a time. We know that giving commands one at a time is difficult and requires a great deal of patience on your part. But to give more than one command at a time to a child with ADHD is to set him up for failure.

8. When I give a command or instruction to my child, am I being specific about what I want him to do?

Vague commands usually lead to lots of compliance problems. *Be specific* about what it is you want your child to do. It is also important to try to give "go" commands whenever possible, rather than "stop" commands. That is, when your child misbehaves, try to tell him what to do instead of the misbehavior, rather than simply telling him to stop the misbehavior.

9. Am I expecting too much too soon?

Above all, whenever you do decide to use a behavior change program, you need to be patient. Do not expect changes overnight. We recommend that whenever you begin a behavior management program, you keep it in place for at least 2 to 3 weeks in order to test its effectiveness. Many parents are tempted to give up on a particular program if their child's behavior does not improve right away. Remember that it takes time to change behavior permanently. So, once you start a program, give it some time to work. If there is no change after 2 or 3 weeks, some modifications in the program may be necessary. If your child's behavior continues to be problematic after you have adjusted the program, or if you feel uncomfortable attempting to handle certain behavior problems, you may want to seek further help from a mental health professional who specializes in working with children who have ADHD.

Can you give a case example that shows how the parenting techniques can be combined into a behavior change program?

We were hoping you would ask this! Let's look again at the case of Barry, who was introduced in chapter 3. As you may recall, Barry was a 7-year-old who did not obey his parents' requests or follow their instructions as well as they would have liked. Barry's parents realized that this problem had been troubling them for some time, so they thought carefully about the behavior they would like to substitute for Barry's noncompliance. The answer was fairly obvious— rather than not doing as they said, Barry's parents wanted Barry to *do as they asked the very first time.*

The next thing Barry's parents did was to chart how frequently Barry obeyed their requests and how often he failed to do so. With a ratio chart, they determined that Barry obeyed an average of 50 percent of his parents' requests during the week.

Next, Barry's parents sat down with their child and told him that his frequent failure to do as they asked was a serious family problem. Things would go a lot better in the home, they said, if Barry stopped that misbehavior and instead started to do what he was asked the very first time. Remembering to be very specific during this discussion, the parents gave Barry numerous examples illustrating how they would like him to behave in the future.

Barry's parents then reviewed the instructions for parents on giving good commands to a child with ADHD. They became careful to give commands that were very clear, very specific, and expressed in a pleasant manner. They made sure to give Barry a command in the form of a direct instruction, rather than in the form of a question. They also made sure they had Barry's attention before giving him a command, and they concentrated on giving him only one command at a time.

In addition to working on Barry's compliance, his parents began to use a star chart for reinforcing overall appropriate behavior in the home. They worked hard to catch his good behavior at least five to eight times a day. Barry's parents then added the positive behavior of "obeying parent commands the very first time" to the list of things Barry could do to add a star to his chart. The parents decided on a daily reward of 25 cents for Barry if he earned at least five stars for that day. A trip to McDonald's would be Barry's weekly reward if he reached his weekly goal of a 55 percent compliance rate. Whenever Barry achieved his weekly compliance rate goal, his parents raised it by 5 to 10 percent in order to slowly increase the demands of his program.

With the use of the star chart, Barry's parents noticed an improvement in his compliance. However, he did continue to ignore their requests whenever he was busy watching TV or playing a game. Consequently, the parents decided that a system was needed for times when Barry was noncompliant with their commands. It would not be wise for them to ignore the misbehavior because this would only teach Barry that he could get away with disobedience.

Barry's parents first decided to use a logical consequence whenever Barry failed to obey their commands. For example, when he did not put his toys away after using them (as specified in the household rules list that his parents had posted in the family room), the toys were locked up for a couple of days. When he failed to hang up his coat in the closet when he came home from school (also an item on the rules list), he was required to hang up all of the family coats for a couple of days.

Although the use of logical consequences did help increase Barry's level of compliance, his parents found it difficult to come up with a suitable logical consequence for many instances of noncompliance. Consequently, they also began to use the time-out procedure.

Barry's parents continued to keep behavior charts and to review them every week to see whether Barry's obedient behavior was increasing and his disobedient behavior decreasing. As his behavior improved to a level with which his parents were pleased, they chose to begin working more specifically on another behavior problem. However, they continued periodically to catch his good behavior at times when he was obedient to their commands and instructions.

Of course, throughout the behavior change process, Barry's parents remembered to give him Very Special Time each day. This helped to change the negative pattern of behavioral interactions between the parents and their child. This change, in turn, increased the chances that Barry's parents would be successful in helping him to improve his overall behavior in the home.

Organizations and Resources for Attention Deficit Hyperactivity Disorder

Children with Attention Deficit Disorders (CHADD)

National Headquarters
499 N.W. 70th Avenue
Suite 308
Plantation, FL 33317
(305) 587-3700

Attention Deficit Disorders Association (ADDA)

National Headquarters
8091 S. Ireland Way
Aurora, CO 80016
(303) 690-0694

ADDA Support Group Hotline

(800) 487-2282

Challenge: A Newsletter of the Attention Deficit Disorder Association

Editor
P.O. Box 2001
West Newbury, MA 01985
(508) 462-0495

Learning Disabilities Association of America

National Headquarters
4156 Library Road
Pittsburgh, PA 15234
(412) 341-1515

Recording Forms

Frequency Chart

Name _____

Week of _____

Appropriate behavior	Sunday	Monday	Tuesday	Wednesday	Thursday	Friday	Saturday
Total appropriate behaviors							

Weekly average of appropriate behavior = _____ (total frequency) ÷ _____ (number of days) = _____ times per day.

Inappropriate behavior							
Total inappropriate behaviors							

Weekly average of inappropriate behavior = _____ (total frequency) ÷ _____ (number of days) = _____ times per day.

Name _____

Duration Chart

Week of _____

Behavior	Sunday	Monday	Tuesday	Wednesday	Thursday	Friday	Saturday

Weekly average = _____ (total minutes) ÷ _____ (number of days) = _____ average number of minutes per day.

Ratio Chart

Name _____

Week of _____

Appropriate behavior	Sunday	Monday	Tuesday	Wednesday	Thursday	Friday	Saturday
Total appropriate behaviors							
Inappropriate behavior							
Total inappropriate behaviors							
Daily percentage (appropriate behaviors per day ÷ total behaviors per day)							

Weekly compliance ratio = _____ (total appropriate behaviors ÷ total behaviors recorded) = _____ %.

Catch Your Child's Good Behavior Star Chart

Name _____   Week of _____

Sunday	
Monday	
Tuesday	
Wednesday	
Thursday	
Friday	
Saturday	

Star Chart for Specific Behaviors

Name _____   Week of _____

	Sunday	Monday	Tuesday	Wednesday	Thursday	Friday	Saturday
Appropriate behavior							
Total appropriate behaviors							
Inappropriate behavior							
Total inappropriate behaviors							
Daily percentage (appropriate behaviors per day ÷ total behaviors per day)							

Weekly compliance ratio = _____ (total appropriate behaviors ÷ total behaviors recorded) = _____ %.

Good Commands/Poor Commands Record

Date _____   Time _____

Good command	Poor command

Compliance With Commands Record

Date _____   Time _____

Complied with command	Disobeyed command

Behavior Contract

I, _____, agree to perform the
following behavior:

_____

_____

_____

_____

_____

If I am successful in performing this behavior, then I will receive:

_____

_____

_____

_____

_____

If I am unsuccessful in performing this behavior, then I will not receive:

_____

_____

_____

_____

_____

I agree to follow the terms of this contract the best I can.

Signature _____   Date _____
             (teenager)

Signature _____   Date _____
             (parent)

Daily Home Report Cards

Sample A (for overall behavior)

Child's name _____ Date _____

Daily rating (circle)

very poor   excellent

1   2   3   4   5

Teacher's signature _____

Sample B (for overall behavior)

Child's name _____ Date _____

Morning rating (circle)   **Afternoon rating (circle)**

very poor   excellent   very poor   excellent

1   2   3   4   5   1   2   3   4   5

Teacher's signature _____

Sample C (for specific behaviors)

Child's name _____ Date _____

Behavior   **Rating**

very poor   excellent

1. _____   1   2   3   4   5
2. _____   1   2   3   4   5

Teacher's signature _____

Bibliography and References

Overviews of ADHD

American Psychiatric Association. (1987). *Diagnostic and statistical manual of mental disorders* (3rd ed., rev.). Washington, DC: Author.

Barkley, R. A. (1990). *Attention Deficit Hyperactivity Disorder: A handbook for diagnosis and treatment.* New York: Guilford.

Conners, C. K., & Wells, K. C. (1986). *Hyperkinetic children: A neuropsychological approach.* Newbury Park, CA: Sage.

LaGreca, A. M., & Quay, H. C. (1984). Behavior disorders of children. In N. S. Endler & J. M. Hunt (Eds.), *Personality and the behavior disorders.* New York: Wiley.

Safer, D. J., & Allen, R. P. (1976). *Hyperactive children.* Baltimore, MD: University Park Press.

Szatmari, P., Offord, D. R., & Boyle, M. H. (1989). Ontario Child Health Study: Prevalence of Attention Deficit Disorder with Hyperactivity. *Journal of Child Psychology and Psychiatry, 30,* 219–230.

Trites, R. L., Dugas, F., Lynch, G., & Ferguson, B. (1979). Incidence of hyperactivity. *Journal of Pediatric Psychology, 4,* 179–188.

Treatments for ADHD

Barkley, R. A. (1977). A review of stimulant drug research with hyperactive children. *Journal of Child Psychology and Psychiatry, 18,* 137–165.

Barkley, R. A. (1988). Attention Deficit Disorder with Hyperactivity. In E. J. Mash & L. G. Terdal (Eds.), *Behavioral assessment of childhood disorders.* New York: Guilford.

Camp, B. W., & Bash, M. A. (1981). *Think aloud: Increasing social and cognitive skills—A problem-solving program for children.* Champaign, IL: Research Press.

Horn, W. F., & Ialongo, N. (1988). Multimodal treatment of Attention Deficit Hyperactivity Disorder in children. In H. E. Fitzgerald, B. M. Lester, & M. W. Yogman (Eds.), *Theory and Research in Behavioral Pediatrics, 4,* 175–220.

Horn, W. F., Ialongo, N., Greenberg, G., Packard, T., & Smith-Winberry, C. (1990). The additive effects of behavioral parent training and self-control therapy with Attention Deficit Hyperactivity Disordered children. *Journal of Clinical Child Psychology, 19,* 98–110.

Horn, W. F., Ialongo, N., Pascoe, J. M., Greenberg, G., Packard, T., Lopez, M., Wagner, A., & Puttler, L. (1991). Additive effects of psychostimulants, parent training, and self-control therapy with ADHD children. *Journal of the American Academy of Child and Adolescent Psychiatry, 30*(2), 233–240.

Horn, W. F., Ialongo, N., Popovich, S., & Peradotto, D. (1987). Behavioral parent training and cognitive-behavioral self-control therapy with ADD-H children: Comparative and combined effects. *Journal of Clinical Child Psychology, 16,* 57–68.

Kendall, P. C., & Braswell, L. (1985). *Cognitive-behavioral therapy for impulsive children.* New York: Guilford.

Meichenbaum, D. (1977). *Cognitive-behavior modification: An integrative approach.* New York: Plenum.

Behavior Management Approaches

Becker, W. C. (1971). *Parents are teachers: A child management program.* Champaign, IL: Research Press.

Blechman, E. A. (1985). *Solving child behavior problems at home and at school.* Champaign, IL: Research Press.

Goldstein, S., & Goldstein, M. (1986). *A parent's guide: Attention Deficit Disorders in children.* Salt Lake City, UT: Neurology, Learning & Behavior Center.

Goldstein, S., & Goldstein, M. (1987). *A teacher's guide: Attention Deficit Disorders in children.* Salt Lake City, UT: Neurology, Learning & Behavior Center.

Patterson, G. R. (1975). *Families: Applications of social learning to family life.* Champaign, IL: Research Press.

Patterson, G. R. (1976). *Living with children: New methods for parents and teachers.* Champaign, IL: Research Press.

Patterson, G. R., & Forgatch, M. (1987). *Parents and adolescents living together. Part 1: The basics.* Eugene, OR: Castalia.

Ross, A. O. (1981). *Child behavior therapy: Principles, procedures, and empirical basis.* New York: Wiley.

Index

About the Authors

Dr. Gregory S. Greenberg is a psychologist in private practice in Everett, Washington, and is also staff psychologist and co-chair of the Psychiatry/Psychology Division of the combined medical staff at General Hospital Medical Center and Providence Hospital, also in Everett. He specializes in evaluating and treating children with ADHD in his private practice. Among his other professional experiences, he has served as coordinator of the Child Behavior Project, a clinical research program at Michigan State University for the treatment of children with ADHD, and as treatment and research consultant for the Parenting Clinic at the University of Washington in Seattle. Dr. Greenberg earned his Ph.D. in child/family clinical psychology and has spoken extensively on the topic of ADHD among school psychologists and other professional groups.

Dr. Wade F. Horn is Chief of the Children's Bureau and Commissioner of the Administration for Children, Youth and Families in the United States Department of Health and Human Services (DHHS). He came to DHHS from Children's Hospital National Medical Center in Washington, D.C., where he was director of outpatient psychological services and vice chair of the Department of Pediatric Psychology. Prior to that, Dr. Horn was an assistant professor of psychology at Michigan State University, as well as associate director of the psychological clinic and director of the specialty clinic in pediatric psychology there. He received his Ph.D. in clinical child psychology and has contributed numerous articles to the journal literature on the topic of ADHD in children.